Temperament

Temperament

The Idea That Solved Music's Greatest Riddle

Stuart Isacoff

Alfred A. Knopf, New York

2002

THIS IS A BORZOI BOOK
PUBLISHED BY ALFRED A. KNOPF

Copyright © 2001 by Stuart Isacoff
All rights reserved under International and Pan-American
Copyright Conventions. Published in the United States by Alfred A.
Knopf, a division of Random House, Inc., New York, and
simultaneously in Canada by Random House of Canada Limited,
Toronto. Distributed by Random House, Inc., New York.
www.aaknopf.com

Grateful acknowledgment is made to the following for
permission to reprint previously published material:

Harvard University Press: Excerpt from a Confucian ode,
interpreted by Ezra Pound, from *Shih-Ching: The Classic Anthology
Defined by Confucius* by Ezra Pound (Cambridge, Mass.: Harvard
University Press), copyright © 1954 by the President and Fellows of
Harvard College. Reprinted by permission of
Harvard University Press.

Selden Rodman: "The Poet" by Rainer Maria Rilke, translated by
Selden Rodman, from *100 Modern Poems,* edited by Selden Rodman
(New York: Pellegrini & Cudahy, 1949). Reprinted by
permission of Selden Rodman.

Knopf, Borzoi Books, and the colophon are registered
trademarks of Random House, Inc.

Library of Congress Cataloging-in-Publication Data
Isacoff, Stuart.
Temperament : the idea that solved music's greatest riddle /
Stuart Isacoff.
p.   cm.
Includes bibliographical references and index.
ISBN 0-375-40355-8 (alk. paper)
1. Musical temperament.   2. Musical intervals and scales.
3. Music—Philosophy and aesthetics   I. Title.
ML 3809.I83 2001
784.192'8—dc21   2001033805

Manufactured in the United States of America
Published November 22, 2001
Reprinted Twice
Fourth Printing, October 2002

To the lights of my life,
Adrienne, Nora, and Rachel

Stuart Isacoff provides examples of the music and tunings he describes in *Temperament*'s Online Audio Companion located at
www.aaknopf.com/authors/isacoff.

Contents

Temperament

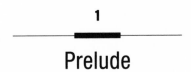

Prelude

Ay me! what warbles yields mine instrument!
The basses shriek as though they were amiss!

—William Percy, "Coelia" (1594)

The piano is perhaps the most generous instrument ever invented. Its range, from bass to treble, is as large as an orchestra's. It allows ten tones—sometimes even more—to be struck simultaneously, and holds them in the air at a pianist's will. The piano can growl and sing and beat time. It can render arid fugues and impressionist waterfalls with equal naturalness. And, unlike the ungrateful French horn or the finicky oboe, if you keep it in tune, it will be an obedient servant. But the principle that truly underlies the piano's versatility is hidden beneath the geometry of its white and black keys.

Clusters of two blacks, then three, then two, and so on, form a repeating pattern above a solid row of whites. When one's eye has become accustomed to the terrain, the alternating groupings signal the names of each note on the keyboard. There are only twelve different tones (each tied to a letter of the alphabet), and in our modern tuning they are built in equidistant steps, like a well-made ladder.

This arrangement produces wondrous results: Through it, a Chopin prelude can gently weep across the keys; Debussy's perfumed phrases can swirl in gentle clouds; Webern can set in motion intricate strings of melody, like threads of glistening pearls.

All of this is possible only because the modern keyboard is a design in perfect symmetry—each pitch is reliably, unequivocally equidistant from the ones that precede and follow it. This tuning allows a musical pattern begun on one note to be duplicated when starting on any other; it creates a musical universe in which the relationships between musical tones are reliably, uniformly consistent. Playing a piano for which this was not true would be like playing a game of chess in which the rules changed from moment to moment.

Yet, that is precisely what many European musicians practicing before the nineteenth century demanded of their instruments. In fact, for hundreds of years, suggestions that our modern system be used were taken as a call to battle: Musicians, craftsmen, church officials, heads of state, and philosophers fought heatedly against the introduction of this *equal-temperament* tuning as something both unnatural and ugly. When Galileo's father, Vincenzo Galilei, supported it as an ideal as early as 1581, he promptly became embroiled in a feud with Gioseffo Zarlino, one of the most influential music theorists of the day. (Sensing a good thing, Chu Tsai-yü, a prince of the Ming dynasty, soon after attributed the concept to the work of Huai Nan Tzu in 122 B.C.E.)

The seventeenth-century instrument-maker Jean Denis—

an advisor to Father Marin Mersenne, philosopher René Descartes's most trusted authority on science and math—rejected today's approach as "quite wretched." Denis's *Treatise on Harpsichord Tuning* was published in 1643, the year that a pupil of Galileo's, Evangelista Torricelli, conducted world-shaking experiments in atmospheric pressure, overturning essential elements of medieval cosmology. Though radical changes in worldview were erupting all around him, Denis remained steadfastly loyal to an old tuning system in which the musical distances between notes were determinedly inconsistent, forming a minefield of "wolf sounds" on his keyboard—notes so dissonant they reminded listeners of the howling of wolves.

Harpsichords and organs (precursors of the piano) thus tuned were capable of producing harmonies of magical, uncorrupted sweetness in one moment and—as musicians attempted to duplicate them while navigating the spans of their keyboards—of earsplitting clashes the next. Composers were prisoners of these torturous practicalities, as were vocalists and instrumentalists who tried to join in. Yet the resistance to a remedy that we find perfectly acceptable today—the tuning of equal temperament—was so powerful, the idea was for generations almost unspeakable.

The crux of the problem can be traced to the ancient Greeks, who defined music's most beautiful sounds as arising from inviolable mathematical relationships—the fingerprints of the gods. These were the proportions through which two separate tones could entwine to form a delightful union. Centuries after Pythagoras conceived of the notion, the great astronomer and music theorist Johannes Kepler restated the idea eloquently: "Geometry existed before the creation, is coeternal with the mind of God, is God himself. . . ." Musical harmony was that geometry made sensual, and was not to be toyed with. And yet . . .

As the art of music evolved, a startling paradox arose that threatened to undermine the entire arrangement. When harpsichords or organs were tuned so that they could consistently produce sounds corresponding to *one* of the venerable formulas, they were rendered incapable of playing the others. No instrument with fixed, unbending notes such as a piano can accommodate them all. Thus, certain combinations of tones that should have sounded sweet and placid could, on an early keyboard instrument, become sour and ragged. In search of a solution, musicians began to *temper,* or alter, their instrument's tunings away from the ancient ideals. The final solution—today's equal temperament—abandoned most of the revered musical proportions altogether.

Acceptance did not come easily. Critics claimed the resulting music had been robbed of its beauty and emotional impact; supporters countered that since all things are subjective, human ears and minds would learn to adapt. The arguments, however, went well beyond musical aesthetics. Equal temperament represented an assault on an idea that had gripped thinkers in nearly every field as a powerful metaphor for a universe ruled by mathematical law.

Saint Augustine found in music's magical proportions God's revealed plan for the building of his churches. Renaissance philosophers sought in them the secrets of obtaining life from the heavens; composers yearned for the power they had bestowed on ancient musicians to tame wild beasts, seduce the celestial spirits, even lure trees to the surface from beneath the sheltering earth. Kepler found in music's time-honored proportions the rules governing the motion of planets in the sky. And Isaac Newton matched the relationships these proportions established between pitches in a musical scale to the arrangement of colors formed by sunlight passing through a prism.

Music's prized proportions permeated not only the inner sanctums of the church, but the workshops of great artists like Filippo Brunelleschi and Leonardo da Vinci. They became entangled in the world of scientific inquiry—engaging the imaginations of such luminaries as Galileo, Kepler, Descartes, Newton, and Christiaan Huygens. They fed debates between the French encyclopedists, challenging the rhetorical skills of Denis Diderot, Jean-Jacques Rousseau, Jean d'Alembert, and Jean-Philippe Rameau on questions such as "What is 'art'?" "What is 'truth'?" and "What is 'natural'?"

They spurred strange musical inventions from remarkable figures like the sixteenth-century avant-garde composer Nicola Vicentino, Mersenne, and Juan Caramuel y Lobkowitz, a Spanish mathematician, professor of theology, and military engineer at the court of Ferdinand III in Prague. And they instigated the creation of countless tuning systems in an incessant negotiation between the old ways and the forces of change. Along the way, they pointed up the conceits and follies of generations of theologians, musicians, philosophers, and scholars who insisted that the proportions in the mind of God must fit in the mind of man.

The general acceptance of equal temperament led to some of the most exquisite music ever written. Why the resistance to it lasted so long, and how it was gradually overcome, is a story that encompasses the most crucial elements of Western culture—social history, religion, philosophy, art, science, economics, and musical evolution—during a period when Europe was struggling to give birth to the modern age. This book tells that story.

It is a tale that includes "temperament" in all its diverse meanings: from the elements that shape the *temperament,* or character, of pivotal thinkers; to endless efforts to *temper*—or transform—the material world into something more desirable; to the practice of *tempering,* or altering, the purest, most beautiful harmonies, following the startling revelation that in certain situations they must be reshaped or they will transform music, Jekyll-and-Hyde-like, into something grotesque.

This last definition, though arcane sounding, marks a profound moment in cultural history. Temperaments, settling like tracks along the winding path of Western civilization, unfettered the engine of musical progress. Once freed, and fueled by the sparks of those most human of qualities— imagination and passion—musical art, with religion, politics, and science in tow, chugged its way inescapably toward our own era.

2

Newton's Desires

But the priest desires. The philosopher desires.

. . . .

And not to have is the beginning of desire . . .

. . . .

It knows that what it has is what is not
And throws it away like a thing of another time,
As morning throws off stale moonlight and shabby
  sleep.

—Wallace Stevens, "Notes Toward a Supreme Fiction"

If students at Trinity College, Cambridge, had an inkling of the dramatic changes Isaac Newton would effect on the shape of history, they gave no sign of it. Indeed, by all appearances, the mere presence of their enigmatic teacher—a lean figure cloaked in scarlet robes, his craggy features gently cradled by an extravagant mass of billowing silver hair—could prompt a general retreat. Almost from the start of his tenure as Trinity's Lucasian Professor of Mathematics, in fact, the greatest scientific mind of the age delivered his lectures, diligently, to a deserted room.

He was the perennial outsider. Even the Crown's best scientists greeted Newton's early pronouncements with stunning disregard. How could they accept his claim, for example, that white light—that cleanest, clearest vapor of illumination, a symbol of heavenly purity—is actually an untidy amalgam of all the colors of the rainbow? His work was dazzling, but it went utterly against the grain.

And so did the man. Socially awkward, self-absorbed, and apparently humorless—the only recorded instance of his having laughed was in response to a question about what use there is in studying Euclid—Newton was driven with a zeal that would unnerve the most devoted scholar: experimenting for days without food or sleep; staring at the sun until the image continued to burn unrelievedly in his head; probing his eye with a darning needle to investigate optical effects. He set out to test the limits of the physical world and in the process often discovered his own.

Nothing was considered beyond the bounds of scrutiny. One day, with burners and flasks and an array of chemicals, Newton coaxed into formation what he believed to be the legendary "philosophical mercury," coveted by sorcerers for its power to transmute gold. As he held it in his gaze, the agent seemed eerily alive. It licked and enveloped a piece of the precious metal, then began to swell and "spring forth into sprouts and branches, changing colors." This was a dangerous activity; in mid-seventeenth-century England, alchemy was considered even more serious than heresy—a hanging offense.

Yet, had Newton paid attention to such prohibitions,

the world would never have received his most celebrated achievement, the theory of gravity. Just such secret moments, spent entreating nature to yield her secrets, enabled him to declare the universe a place in which all things embrace each other, even across the vast distances of space. It changed everything.

In the years following the publication of his idea, the theme of gravitation soared through European culture like a great mythical bird. It roosted in the writings of political observers, who began to applaud efficient monarchies for their ability to attract bodies to a center. It touched the world of high-handed religious philosophers, who imparted a Newtonian luster to their treatises by crafting phrases like "velocities of suspicion" and calculating the ratio between the highest possible earthly happiness and the bliss of heaven. Composer Jean-Philippe Rameau explained the directional pull of tonal harmonies and was dubbed "the Newton of music." In the end, so breathtaking was the scope of his influence that, following Newton's death, there was talk of reforming the calendar to mark 1642—the year of his birth—as the beginning of time.

As Trinity's Lucasian Professor, however, he was a man whose efforts—and demeanor—were often simply unfathomable. Spiritual quests are a lonesome business, particularly in a town castigated by Charles I for its excessive fondness for taverns and student liaisons with "women of mean estate and of no good fame." Newton's archrival, Robert Hooke, steadfastly defended Cambridge's randy tradition in taverns and coffeehouses; enjoyed the company of several mistresses, including his niece and ward, Grace; even, with impressive scientific fervor, recorded his orgasms in a diary.

Temperament

Newton had passions of another sort. As his contemporary the poet John Milton wrote of a "Paradise regained" through the rejection of worldly temptation, the monkish Newton busily sought his own version of lost splendor—a key once held by ancient magicians and seers. He burned with a desire to uncover it: the mysterious, invisible system of the universe.

And so, duties dispatched, Newton would withdraw to the far side of the school's Great Court like a storm-crossed ship headed to port. There, in the shadow of Trinity's stately chapel, he kept his rooms and, below them, a small, modest-looking wooden structure that housed his laboratory. Within those cramped walls, Newton searched for new ways to unlock the wonders of nature.

Pursuing subjects as diverse as optics, biblical revelation, alchemy, and planetary motion, Newton sought the thread that would connect them all. It was while studying the behavior of light that he came upon what he believed to be an important link. While projecting the sun's rays through a refracting prism, he had his assistant carefully chart the distances between the strongest colors. Something about their placement caught his attention: The spacing of colors in the spectrum seemed to imitate the proportional "distances" between the tones in a musical scale.

For Newton, the finding was rich in implications about the ether through which nature's forces move. But his comparison of the natural boundaries within a rainbow to the building blocks of music harbored a nagging riddle, one that, even after centuries of debate, was still confounding the greatest talents of his generation. Newton had been intrigued by it from his earliest student days: the paradox of

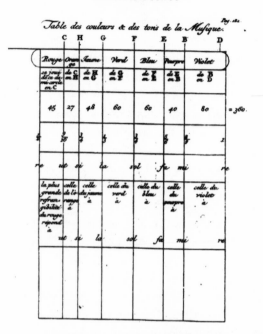

Newton's spectrum-scale, matching colors to musical tones, as shown in Voltaire's *Elémens de la philosophie de Neuton* (1738)

musical tunings. As much as arguments over the motion of the planets or the cause of the ocean's tides, this issue had embroiled philosophers, theologians, mathematicians, and musicians in an often rancorous dispute over the nature of the physical world.

At bottom was a deceptively simple question: Had nature created laws for melody and harmony as it had for hues of light? The medieval universities, tracing the matter back to the ancient Greeks, had claimed it had, and taught music as invisible architecture, a mirror of the heavens. "Without music, there can be no perfect knowledge," wrote the medieval encylopedist Isidore of Seville. "For even the universe is said to have been put together with a certain harmony of sounds."

Musical tones are vibrations—of strings sent rippling by the pluck of a quill or the caress of a bow; of hollow tubes shivering around a current of wind; of gongs stunned into sound by the blow of a mallet. As they travel through the air to our ears and excite our minds, we perceive these tones in patterns of high and low, and find their entwining beautiful—or noxious. To the ancient thinkers, harmonies—combinations of two or more tones sounding simultaneously—were pleasing to a man's ears and soul only when their constituent vibrations met in certain simple, divinely inspired mathematical ratios. Euphony—beauteous sound—was a special kind of number.

Today, as in the ancient world, we hear a magical resonance when two notes vibrate together in one of those simple proportions: when the frequency of the top tone is twice that of the bottom one, for example. Or when the rates of their vibrations form the ratio three to two. Tones joined in these relations are known as *concordances*. They announce to our ears a sense of completeness and of inevitability: They belong together.

Play the well-known scale *do-re-mi-fa-sol-la-ti-do:* The top and bottom *do*s, if isolated from the rest, merge effortlessly, as though one were a continuation of the other. The same effect results when any two *res*, *mis*, or *fas* are sounded simultaneously. In each of these cases the higher tone (an *octave* above the lower one) is vibrating twice as fast. Or play *do* and *sol* (the fifth note of the scale that begins on *do*) together. In this case, the higher tone is vibrating three times for every two vibrations of the lower one, and the ear perceives a joyful agreement between the two.

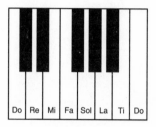

For centuries these auditory experiences served as corroboration of immutable natural law—affirmed by theological as well as musical authority. But as music evolved a palette of complex harmonies and intricate textures, and instruments with fixed pitches (like lutes and keyboards) came into prominence, something unexpected happened: The unchangeable harmonic formulas seemed to falter. As it turns out, the strings of a piano, or of its earlier incarnation the harpsichord, may be tuned so that any one of the cherished ratios can be rendered perfectly throughout the range of the instrument. A *do* can be put in tune with every other *do,* for example; a *re* in tune with every other *re.* Each of these tones on the keyboard can be set to vibrate exactly twice as fast as the like-named partner below it.

However, the musical tones that will produce those perfect 2:1 relationships across the keyboard are different from the ones needed to create perfect 3:2 relationships. So, making all the *octaves* (the distance from *do* to *do*) "pure" guaran-

Temperament

tees that all the *fifths* (the distance from *do* to *sol,* or *re* to *la*) can't be. Remarkably, these (and other) long-revered musical proportions refuse to keep company: When multiplied, their various progeny threaten to collide abrasively, as if there were a curvature in musical space.

Since only a limited number of concords could be preserved, some keys on the instrument could be rendered useless. Harpsichords came to resemble at times the singer whose voice cracks when she tries to execute a particular musical figure. Long before Newton's day, musicians had initiated schemes to address this problem, most often through slight alterations (called temperings) in the formulas used to create those cherished harmonies.

Nevertheless, by the mid–seventeenth century, the problem was reaching new heights. Robert Burton's monumental survey of the range of human moods, *The Anatomy of Melancholy,* was a best-seller, reflecting the age's growing delight in probing the "comedies and tragedies . . . misery and madness" of the mortal condition. Composers, seeking to provoke the human passions—whether sadness, tenderness, rage, heroism, or wonder—moved beyond the bounds of past practices, filling their instrumental pieces with bold leaps and dramatic contrasts, making greater demands on the instruments themselves. Through complexity, innovation, and a striving for effect, the musical landscape had shifted. Once-gentle harmonies, moving into new positions across the keyboard, became caught in the bowels of an inflexible tuning system, and produced a sound so harsh the result was compared to the wails of a wild animal.

Music's invisible building blocks—the magical numbers defining sonic beauty—were increasingly like great, ethereal forms that had lost their bearings. It was as if the stately pyramids had been transplanted to hilly terrain, their bases toppling over helplessly, their points obtruding at odd, ugly angles.

Unsatisfied with half-measures, some musicians turned to a radical solution—shaving and padding the foundations of those pyramids to set them aright on the new, rocky ground. They abandoned the accepted musical formulas altogether and completely reconfigured the keyboard's tuning—replacing its complicated labyrinth of uneven steps and shifting proportions with an octave span (*do* to *do*) neatly divided into twelve equal parts. This was akin to taking a file to the pieces of a particularly frustrating jigsaw puzzle in order to force their irregular shapes into submission. The result—our modern system (known as twelve-tone equal temperament) of twelve perfectly uniform musical steps—was regarded by many as repugnant, even catastrophic: a violation of nature. Before long, opposing camps were hurling insults at each other over the issue, and scrambling for political leverage.

Cardinal Francesco Barberini, nephew of Pope Urban VIII, found himself in the middle of one notorious skirmish over the matter in 1640—a fight between renowned composer and organist Girolamo Frescobaldi and Barberini's former secretary, the scholar Giovanni Battista Doni. Doni, onetime secretary to the sacred College of Cardinals, was—in his own view—too mild-mannered for life among the prelates, and had withdrawn to the post of professor of rhetoric at the University of Florence. His reaction to the new tuning was, however, anything but gentle.

The argument broke out over the treatment of a majestic

organ in the basilica of San Lorenzo in Damaso. Cardinal Barberini held court as Frescobaldi, one of the greatest virtuosos of his day, defended the efficacy of the new approach; Doni, the true believer, recoiled in horror at the prospect of abandoning the organ to such a horrible fate, and of the bad reputation that would befall Roman musicians for allowing it.

Though Barberini eventually sided with Doni, the perturbed orator, shaken by the close call, continued to wage war on behalf of the old guard. Poor Frescobaldi, he accused, had been tricked into turning against his own better judgment by means of generous and free-flowing libations. (Frescobaldi was easily attacked on such grounds, his reputation for impetuousness having been established after an incident with a certain Angiolina in Rome.) To make matters worse, claimed Doni, the composer was actually so unlearned he often had to ask the advice of his wife!

In an effort to sidestep the controversy, instrument makers proposed the creation of keyboards with extra keys, so performers would have more than the usual number of choices for finding a note with the proper proportion. It was a cumbersome solution, and equally disputatious. One contest between rival organ builders took place in 1684 as Bernard Smith and Renatus Harris each vied for the right to install his instrument in London's Temple Church. Smith—who designed his organ with more options by splitting certain keys down the middle—engaged two of the most formidable composers and performers of his day, John Blow and Henry Purcell, to demonstrate it. For his part, Harris employed the queen's organist, Giovanni Battista Draghi. The competition was fierce—so fierce that Harris's followers sabotaged Smith's organ the night before the trial by cutting its bellows.

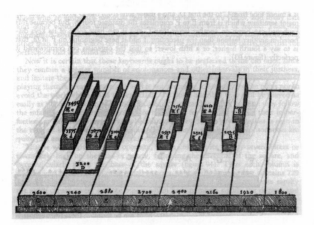

A musical keyboard with nineteen keys to the octave, from Marin
Mersenne's *Harmonie universelle* (1636–37)

Advocates persisted. As late as 1768, composer George
Frideric Handel paid for an organ with split keys for the
Foundling Hospital in London. Nevertheless, these complicated musical inventions found little acceptance. And so the
conflict remained.

It germinated far beyond musical circles. In science and
philosophy, the argument over musical tuning became a natural point of contention between proponents of abstract reason and those of experience. Descartes was the reigning
thinker before Newton. He had imagined the world as a perfect machine: a great composite of rigidly defined parts (not
unlike his era's lady of fashion who, according to one popular lampoon of the time, "takes herself asunder, when she
goes to bed, into some twenty boxes, and about noon the
next day is put together again like a great German clock").

Music's ratios were gears in a grand design, and Descartes denounced any notion of corrupting their ideal forms. A growing number of pragmatists, however, took a different point of view. And history was shifting in their favor. Newton's revolution was, in fact, merely the crest of a great wave washing over the world of science in favor of observation and practicality.

Arithmetic, geometry, astronomy, and music had been studied in all the great centers of learning as a means for discerning the true essence of the universe, and over the years each had acquired a sizable ballast of theology and convention. In the contest between evidence and authority, authority clearly triumphed. After all, as Plato had warned, the material world is confusing, a realm of variables. It is "always becoming and never is"; better to seek "that which always is and has no becoming."

This argument was the basis for Descartes's insistence that in a perfectly calibrated universe the emptiness of a vacuum was not only inconceivable, but an affront to God the mechanic. Even after Blaise Pascal announced his successful experiments in creating one, Descartes simply dug in his heels and announced that the only vacuum was in Pascal's head. (Pascal paid another, more poignant price for his trailblazing experiments. A vacuum-filled, limitless cosmos turned out to be as existentially unsettling for him as it was for Descartes. "The eternal silence of these infinite spaces frightens me," he confessed.)

A generation earlier, such thinking had blinded even the remarkable Galileo, who suffered at the hands of the inquisitors after calling for a divorce between theology and science. Despite the evidence of telescopic sightings to the contrary,

Galileo reasoned that the orbits of planets must be circles rather than ellipses, because he could not bring himself to shed an old idea of how the cosmos is shaped.

But with the dawning of the scientific age, a new breed of seeker was turning tradition on its head. A Royal Society dedicated to this new approach was launched in England in 1662. The group's motto put the idea succinctly: "Nullius in Verba"—"At the dictation of no one." If experiment disproved official canon, so be it.

Newton, who would eventually become president of the Royal Society, was devoted to the principle. It accounted for his relentless investigations and his disdain for untested hypotheses. It had even prompted his refusal, as a matter of conscience, to take the holy vows required of his professorship. As a result, he had been forced to send a plea to Charles II for permission to keep his job; the king responded with a special dispensation. (In a contentious religious climate, Charles did his utmost to promote what he described as "liberty to tender consciences." Newton's case, of course, offered added incentive: The king had more than a passing interest in experimental science, and had even discovered it useful when wagering on the horses.) Newton was sure of the existence of a divine creator; he just remained unconvinced that God abides by church doctrine.

As the witness of eyes and ears gained the mantle of legitimacy, sense perception—once regarded with deep suspicion—now occupied center stage. Throughout the sciences, new developments took root, and the founding members of the Royal Society often led the way. They included John Wilkins, who entertained guests by producing rainbows in his garden, and Robert Boyle, who studied gems and found from the regular arrangements of their structures evidence for the atomic theory of matter. Robert Hooke, who glimpsed the cellular structure of plants as he peered into a microscope, also determined why stars twinkle, and measured the frequency of a buzzing fly's wings by establishing the musical note it created in flight. After studying the movements of birds in the air, the prolific Hooke designed thirty varieties of flying machines. Joseph Glanvill went a step further, promoting the idea of *effortless* flight through a sixth sense; he reported to the society on a demonstration of telepathy by a former Oxford student who had learned the art from Gypsies.

All were fair game for the satirists. In *Gulliver's Travels* Jonathan Swift depicts them as the Grand Academy of Lagado, whose members formulated plans for extracting sunshine from cucumbers and building houses from the roof downward. Author Samuel Butler parodied their efforts by presenting the image of a club of scientists excited by the discovery of an elephant on the moon—only to find that it was a mouse in their telescope. But a new way of assessing the world had arrived, and with it, a fascination with the act of perceiving.

It was a change already sweeping through the arts. In Italy, the great sculptor Gian Lorenzo Bernini had turned the very idea of perceiving into an exhilarating adventure. His daring theater productions were designed to raise questions about the distinction between what is real and what is unreal; an enthusiastic public rushed to attend, hardly knowing what to expect next. In one of Bernini's milder presentations, a curtain fell to reveal an onstage audience watching another play—a stunning bit of self-referential drama in which the audience was jolted from merely watching a play into watching the act of watching. In another presentation, he arranged for the scenery to catch fire—as if by accident—only to reveal a garden that had been there, hidden all along. Perhaps his greatest spectacle, *The Inundation of the Tiber* featured a mass of water bursting through a dike; the torrent rushed toward a panicking audience, then drained away at the last moment.

Though he used deception to achieve it, Bernini's aim was actually to enhance a sense of the real—to convey the truth more effectively. He explained that in a sculpture of a man in which one hand is raised in the air, that hand would have to be made bigger because the space around it would affect its perceived dimensions; that if someone suddenly turned white he would not seem himself, so when a portrait is created in marble the features must be modified to compensate for the lack of color.

Bernini criticized Michelangelo for failing to make his figures appear as if made of flesh, and bragged that stone was "like pasta" in *his* hands—that he could fashion marble like wax. And indeed he could. His genius for manipulating the act of perception—by altering perspective, or highlighting certain details in a rendering, or using materials and techniques to blur the lines between sculpture and painting—actually allowed Bernini to achieve new levels of authenticity in bringing a scene to life. Art, he taught us, is a kind of trickery.

This use of artifice—so keenly appreciated in the work of Bernini—was at the heart of the long-smoldering controversy in music. If a sculptor could exaggerate human features to make a figure seem more lifelike, why couldn't musicians manipulate those "heaven-sent" musical proportions and still convey sonic beauty? Wasn't it possible, in the end, to alter music's "natural" face and still retain its potent properties?

Faith and pure reason were on one side, practicality on the other. Newton had demonstrated a unique ability to balance reason and evidence: Might he discover a "philosophical mercury" of music, a way of transmuting the ancient proportions so that their valued qualities could permeate the newest type of musical "vessel"? With a mathematician's skill and an alchemist's reach, he set out to find an answer.

Newton had already begun a mathematical analysis of various musical scales in his student days. In a tiny, dogged scrawl his notebooks outline the formulas used to divide the most basic musical span, the octave, into various arrangements of the usual twelve tones; then, in precise columns of numbers, he compared other scales that divide the same span into 20, 24, 25, 29, 36, 41, 51, 53, 100, 120, and 612 parts. To help him make comparisons, Newton created a new mathematical tool—a standard unit for measuring the intervals between notes—nearly two hundred years before acoustical science rediscovered its usefulness.

An unpublished treatise reveals his assessment of the situation. Man is not inherently musical, the distinguished scientist claimed; natural singing is the sole property of birds. In contrast to our feathered friends, humans perform and understand only what they are taught. Nevertheless, Newton insisted, there *is* something wrong with scales based on modern, "contrived" proportions—like those of equal temperament.

Man's senses have become accustomed to the new sounds, wrote Newton, but the alterations of the modernists rob music of its real power. To those who know better, equal temperament's compromised tuning is as ungrateful to the ear as "soiled and faint colors are to the eye." Still, he acknowledged, the proportions "which the God of Nature has fitted" were now impractical. A system in tune with *both* man and heaven was needed.

It was a worthy ideal. Despite Newton's best efforts, however, the controversy would continue to rage for well over a hundred years.

3

In the Realm of the Gods

Apollo, Apollo! Lord of the ways, my ruin.
You have undone me once again, and utterly.

—Aeschylus, *Agamemnon*

The seeds of the dilemma were planted in the hills of ancient Croton, where, around 530 B.C.E., a philosopher named Pythagoras founded a mystical community after retreating from the advance of the Persians into Asia Minor. Settling in what is now southern Italy, at the edge of the spawning culture that radiated from across the Mediterranean Sea, Pythagoras set out not to create a theory of music, but to find the resonance of a life well lived.

The Greek world, brimming with a creative spirit, had already given rise to marvels of human ingenuity. On his native island of Samos, Pythagoras had witnessed an astounding feat of engineering—the tunneling of a nine hundred-yard aqueduct through the hill of Kastro, begun from both ends simultaneously. Meanwhile, his contemporary Theodorus had devised a central heating system for the temple of Diana at Ephesus, and helped usher in a new era of metallurgy by crafting life-size statues in bronze. Astronomical observations had enabled the philosopher Thales to predict a solar eclipse, and aided sailors in their navigation of the seas. And a unique system of self-governance was offering a taste of unparalleled political freedom. As the great philosophers pondered the known world and debated its basic nature, the reach of the human mind must have seemed limitless.

Yet, men's fortunes could be as shifting as the winds over the Aegean. It was impossible to predict the course of natural events—however mightily the oracle at Delphi tried—or to escape the ravages of war. When the fates were unkind, there was little a soul could do. And unkind they could be. For, barely concealed beneath its orderly veneer, Greek civilization harbored a shadow world inhabited by capricious gods and demons who meddled in human affairs, just for the sport of it.

Reasoned equanimity crumbled quickly before great Zeus, who sent rain and lightning; or mighty Poseidon, who stirred the waters and caused the ground to tremble. Such spirits might steel your limbs for battle in one moment and dull your wits in the next. Happy thoughts could arrive by way of owl-faced Athene, but in the blink of an eye bloodsucking Erinys could roil your innards with an uncontrollable infatuation. "What could I do? Deity will always have its way," cried Homer's remorseful Agamemnon in the *Iliad*, after robbing Achilleus of his mistress.

Forceful, unsettling emotions were seen as inexplicable intruders. When Phrynichus produced *The Capture of Miletus* in Athens and moved his audience to tears, the playwright was fined a thousand drachmas for making them unhappy. In a world devoted to reason, to lose oneself—except in the purifying delirium of certain mystic rites—was a sure step to ruin.

And music, with its ability to harness the heart, embodied a force as potent as any Olympian messenger.

As Jason and his Argonauts "smote the swelling brine with their oars, and the surge broke over the oar-blades; and on this side and on that the dark water seethed with spume, foaming terribly under the strokes of the mighty heroes," it was to the musical sound of Orpheus's lyre. When the great warrior Odysseus was reduced to tears, it was not on the battlefield, but through the simple song of a minstrel. Music had the power to beguile. It's no wonder that the great god Apollo received his musical instrument—a tortoiseshell lyre—from Hermes, the trickster thief.

Into these turbulent straits sailed Pythagoras, who accomplished a remarkable feat. He captured the musical voices of the gods.

Like other spiritual leaders of that ancient civilization, Pythagoras advanced a method for taming life's unruly tides. Part mystic, part huckster, part mathematical wizard, he walked the public spaces of Croton in white robes and pants and wore a gold crown, luring followers with the promise of serenity. His program included righteous polity (the equality of men and women, communal ownership), austere living (no eating of beans, speaking obscurely, or sacrificing of white roosters), and contemplation. His cult, and his status, grew to become a dominant force in the region. Before long, witnesses were attributing to him powers of prophecy, miraculous healing, and the ability to journey beyond the confines of his body. He didn't deny it. A century after his death, Empedocles recounted tales of how Pythagoras had magically stayed the winds, restored life to a dead woman, and vanished bodily from the world to become a god. Not surprisingly, he was eventually run out of town. Yet, among the ranks of the great philosophers seeking to uncover the secret nature of the *cosmos* (literally "order"; he was the first to use the term), Pythagoras, the magician-wanderer and purveyor of dark secrets, left perhaps the most lasting imprint.

Many thinkers before him had striven to define the basic stuff of the universe. Thales of Miletus—considered by Aristotle to be the founder of Western philosophy—decided it was water, the life-giver. His successor, and Pythagoras's teacher, Anaximander, claimed it had to be something intangible and boundless: a thing beyond name. Anaximenes concluded it was air; and Heraclitus, struck by nature's unceasing cycles of death and rebirth, insisted it was the great transformative agent fire. Fire takes in sand, Pliny the Elder would later exclaim, giving back "now glass, now silver . . . now pigments, now medicines. By fire stones are melted into bronze, by fire iron is made and mastered, by fire gold is produced. . . ." For Pythagoras, the fundament of the universe was not so coarse a thing as water, fire, or air, nor beyond discovery, but in a category all its own. It was something obvious, yet easy to miss; lacking in body, yet clearly defined; beyond sense, but a fulfillment of all man's perceptions. Through it, the hidden structure of the world became transparent. Pythagoras's primordial substance was number.

The source of this inspiration was Egypt, where Thales had once learned the art of estimating the height of a pyramid through the image it cast on the sands. The Egyptians had long practiced the art of measurement, in the skies and on the ground. As far back as 1000 B.C.E., an Egyptian priest named Ahmes had produced a mathematical guide filled with these secrets of material reality—the Rhind papyrus—with the seductive title "Directions for Knowing All Dark Things."

To the initiate, math was wondrous indeed. A master of the art could unveil remarkable connections between number and shape; he could rule over errant fractions; divide nine loaves among ten men; disclose the subtle rules governing qualities like odd and even. He could discover fascinating arrays of reciprocal relations in which one set of numbers seemed connected to another, as if these symbols were practicing their own clandestine rituals. The thrill of recognition when numbers defined the parts of a figure; the pleasure of certainty when they validated unchanging rules; the mystical awe inspired by the hidden relationships they held with each other—all evidenced their unassailable position in the scheme of the universe.

Pythagoras built on the Egyptian store of knowledge, and imbued numbers with the ability to symbolize every measurable quality, even intangibles like justice and opportunity. He peered beneath the surface of solid lines and found rows of distinguishable points. He discerned unusual mathematical relationships, such as "perfect" numbers equal to the sum of their own divisors—like 6, produced by $1 + 2 + 3$, and 28, which results from $1 + 2 + 4 + 7 + 14$. The Egyptians had already found extraordinary beauty in such special mathematical formulations, such as the "golden" triangle, whose sides are in the proportion 3:4:5. Seduced by such charms,

Plato—who placed a sign over his academy door warning entrants that a background in mathematics was required—later derived the ideal number of citizens in a state, 5,040, by multiplying $1 \times 2 \times 3 \times 4 \times 5 \times 6 \times 7$.

Pythagoras explored triangles and squares, and calculated the famous Pythagorean theorem of right triangles (the sum of the squares of the sides is equal to the square of the hypotenuse)—another victory in the search for divine immutability. He even offered the promise of spiritual escape by tapping number's unwavering essence. His followers were instructed that upon rising from sleep they were to erase the impressions left behind by their forms, as if to become less like (differentiated) human beings and more like (transcendent) number. Number, as his disciple Philolaus would later exclaim, became "great, all-powerful, all-sufficing, the first principle and the guide in the life of gods, of heaven, of men. Without it all is without limit, obscure, indiscernible." To a world in endless flux, Pythagoras bestowed the gift of limit: the fount of invariance.

Ironically, though Pythagoras rejected Heraclitus's view of fire as the primary substance, it was a fiery furnace that afforded him the opportunity to discover his numbers for the unchanging principle in music. "I have seen the blacksmith at his work at the mouth of his furnace, his fingers like the skin of a crocodile; he smells worse than the roe of a fish," wrote an ancient Egyptian commentator. But for Pythagoras, the blacksmith's shop became an altar to beauty. As legend has it, the philosopher of Croton was passing the shop one day when he was gripped by the sounds coming from within. Various hammers striking against anvils were creating a disordered, clanging chorus. Every so often, however, the reverberant clatter would seem to soften and blend into a mellifluous union. Pythagoras was determined to uncover the source of this phenomenon, and he entered the shop to observe.

The hammers were of different weights, and it turned out that each generated its own distinct tone. We can imagine Pythagoras watching as the heavy tools swung against their targets; one instant they produced a raucous mess, the next, a resonant choir. Finally, it dawned on him: Whenever the relative weights of the hammers striking the anvils formed certain simple ratios—when their heavy heads were found to be in the proportions 2:1 or 3:2 or 4:3—the notes they produced together created the most marvelous harmonies: sweet, bell-like, and exquisite.

There was substantiality to those fleeting concordances, as if they were wispy shapes of an unseen world. These were not mere reverberations, but the songs of the sirens, "the music of the spheres"—melodies of an orderly universe. And snaring their proportions with his intellect gave Pythagoras a foothold on music's mysterious power.

Alas, this story is apocryphal. The claim that those agreeable resonances can be produced by controlling the weights of hammerheads plays fast and loose with the laws of acoustics. Nevertheless, the remaining part of the tale is important. As the story goes, Pythagoras duplicated this experience at home—not with varying weights but with differing lengths of string. And here the science is not only solid but profound; indeed, Pythagoras's string experiments created the very foundation of musical art for thousands of years of Western civilization.

A taut string, excited by the friction of a bow, the pluck-

The bottom level of Robert Fludd's *Temple of Music* (1618) depicts Pythagoras entering the blacksmith's shop.

ing of a quill, or the striking of a hammer, will quiver in waves—like the ripples in a pond when a pebble has been tossed in. We hear these rapid undulations as musical tones. Their speed varies according to the length of the string. The shorter the string, the faster the vibrations and the higher the tone. (The amount of tension on the string will also affect its "pitch," or frequency of vibration.)

Every string instrument exploits this phenomenon. As a

violinist runs the hairs of her bow across a string to set it in motion, she selects a spot on the fingerboard with her free hand to control how much of its span will be allowed to vibrate. A guitarist's right hand strums a set of strings, but the fingers on his left hand will choose their lengths by applying pressure at selected frets. Each key on a harpsichordist's instrument triggers the plucking of its own particular string, designed by length and tension to vibrate at a certain frequency; the strings are arrayed like those on a harp, with the longest at one end and successive strands growing ever shorter over the keyboard's compass.

The results will range from low, brassy murmurs—as long, languorous strings are stirred from slumber by the flick of a quill—to high, piercing sounds, like those from a singer's throat tightening to reach a dramatic peak. We sense this stretch between low and high tones as a distance; musicians call it an *interval*. Intervals strung together form melodies; when piled on top of each other they create harmonies.

Pythagoras's discovery was that the most "agreeable" harmonies—those whose tones seem to be "in sync" with each other, like marchers lockstepped to the beat of the same drum—are formed by the simplest kind of mathematical relationships. If the vibrations of one tone are twice as fast as the vibrations of another's, for example, the two will blend so smoothly the result will sound almost like a single entity. The separate constituents of this musical marriage are oscillating in the proportion 2:1. Now suppose one of these partners were to stray—causing the relationship to degenerate from a solid, simple footing of 2:1 into a more complex ratio, say 1.9:1. Viewing a painting or a monument, the eye would

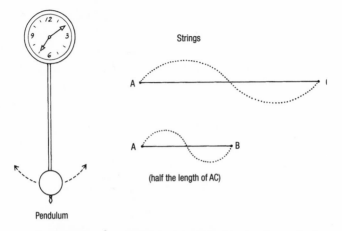

Strings

A ────────────────────────── I

A ──────────── B

(half the length of AC)

Pendulum

The pendulum of a grandfather clock swings at a steady rate fixed by the length of its shaft. Though its motion is less obvious to the naked eye, a vibrating string similarly oscillates side to side or up and down, and its frequency also varies according to length (though different rules apply to free-swinging pendulums and fixed strings). When a string is reduced in size by half, it vibrates twice as fast and sounds an octave higher.

easily tolerate such a tiny shift; the ears, however, would find this new union far less amicable: grating and sour rather than placid. This is, admittedly, an extreme case: The most basic musical ratio, 2:1, is also the one least capable of tolerating deviation. Nevertheless the fact remains: Only through the simplest kind of proportion does a pleasing harmony arise. Complexity breeds chaos.

The proportion 2:1 stands as the first of Pythagoras's special musical relations. Another is the sound of two tones vibrating so that the higher one produces three vibrations for every two of the lower one. The last musical concordance discovered by Pythagoras occurs when the two tones are vibrating in the relationship 4:3.

The science of selecting an instrument's string lengths—and therefore, the musical distances between its tones—begins with Pythagoras's discovery. We can approximate the beautiful musical proportions he found by utilizing the following notes of the piano keyboard.

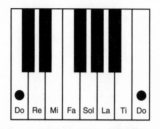

Playing or singing the familiar musical scale *do-re-mi-fa-sol-la-ti-do*, we call the interval, or musical distance, from the left-hand *do* to the *do* above it an *octave* (remember, musical pitches rise as the keyboard extends to the right). Their vibrations are in the ratio 2:1—that is, assuming that the tension and materials used, which will also affect pitch, are the same, the string for the lower *do* would be twice the length of the higher *do;* the lower string vibrates twice as slowly. Intervals can *begin* from any note at all, however; so other octaves found on the piano keyboard include the distances from *re* to *re, mi* to *mi, fa* to *fa,* and so on.

To get an idea of the sound of an octave, think of the opening two notes of the song "Over the Rainbow," beginning on the word "Somewhere." Though a leap separates them, the two *do*s sound so much alike, they share the same name. Listening to them, you might think you are perceiving two reflections of a single object, or two points along the same straight line.

The musical interval called a *perfect fifth* is found by playing or singing the notes *do* to *sol* (or *re* to *la,* or *mi* to *ti*), again progressing rightward. These are the first and fifth notes of the standard musical scale. As in every musical fifth, the *sol* is vibrating faster than the *do* (and their relative string lengths are) in the proportion 3:2. Richard Strauss used this interval for the opening two notes of *Thus Spake Zarathustra* (familiar to movie audiences worldwide as the triumphant theme music of the film *2001: A Space Odyssey*). In the popular folk song "Kumbaya," the first and third notes span the interval of a perfect fifth.

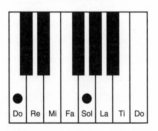

This perfect fifth sounded together as a harmony gives the impression of a melding of complementary parts, a marriage between two willing partners. Its hollow, open sound also suggests two luminous parallel lines, their glow vanquishing the space that separates them. Galileo, thousands of years after the time of Pythagoras, described the effect of this harmony as "a tickling of the eardrum such that its softness is modified with sprightliness, giving at the same moment the impression of a gentle kiss and of a bite."

The interval produced when two notes are vibrating in

(or string lengths form) the ratio 4:3 is called a *perfect fourth*. It can be heard by playing or singing *do* to the *fa* above it (or *re* to *sol,* or *sol* to *do*). Richard Wagner used this fourth for the first two notes of his famous bridal chorus in *Lohengrin* ("Here Comes the Bride"). The popular song "Auld Lang Syne" also begins with this interval.

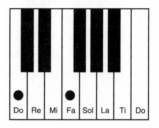

These were music's concordances—the covenants that tones form under heaven's watchful eye. For the Pythagoreans, though, the importance of these special proportions went well beyond music. They were signs of the natural order, like the laws governing triangles; music's rules were simply the geometry governing things in motion: not only vibrating strings but also celestial bodies and the human soul. With each of his formulations, Pythagoras provided inspired solutions to life's questions, and influenced thinkers for thousands of years. He had brought an end to the chaos of a limitless universe—or so it seemed. But concealed deeply within Pythagoras's most famous formulas was a fatal flaw. He knew it, and this knowledge became the great mystery of the Pythagorean cult, to be revealed only upon risk of death.

Here was the secret: Sometimes Pythagorean calculations gave rise to wild, unfathomable numbers—what the Greeks named *alogon,* "the unutterable"; today we call these *incommensurables*—and members of his order were forbidden to disclose their existence. They reveal a world not of containment, but of boundlessness.

An example is the relationship between the diagonal and the side of a square. Pythagoras's rules can be used to calculate the value of any diagonal; but in the case of a square, that calculation will yield an *irrational* number. Such a number—like the square root of 2, for instance—cannot be expressed in the world of integers: It has no definable limit. It simply goes on forever.

In our sophisticated, scientific age of black holes and antimatter, dealing with such entities is child's play. But in the time of Pythagoras their mere existence gave rise to a dangerous universe. The implications were terrifying. If numbers without limit were to exist, lines would have to be infinitely divisible. And if lines were infinitely divisible, they could not be comprised of Pythagoras's discrete, measurable points; his entire philosophy of the physical world would thus be reduced to nonsense. Pythagoras's theorem became, in effect, its own foil, the gateway to a boundless and uncertain universe—but only to those who knew the secret. We are told of the fate that met those who antagonized the gods by letting loose this knowledge in the world: They were, reported Proclos, shipwrecked, to a man.

As it turns out, Pythagoras's musical proportions contain the same kind of flaw. According to legend, the philosopher discovered this himself while measuring musical proportions on an instrument he invented called the monochord. It consists of a single string suspended over a movable bridge; the bridge effectively lengthens or shortens the segment of the string that vibrates. We'll imagine that when he first plucked the open string of a monochord he sounded a *do*. Then, moving the bridge, he located the point along that string from which he could produce the *do* an octave higher. Starting from that new point, he moved the bridge again to find another octave, and then another. One by one, he produced a series of octaves until he had done this seven times.

On another monochord, he followed a similar procedure, but used the movable bridge to divide the string length so that it would sound a fifth above the starting point—creating the span from *do* to *sol*. From that point he moved the bridge along the remaining length of string to form another fifth (from *sol* to *re*), and from the latter point he formed yet another fifth (from *re* to *la*). He did this twelve times. Progressing by perfect fifths in this way, the monochord will go through every one of the twelve different tones (both black and white keys) available on the piano. This progression of fifths moves along a great musical circle before eventually reaching a tone with the same name as the one with which it began. At the end of this experiment, Pythagoras believed he would arrive at the same final *do* on both instruments.

The tones sounded by his two instruments were, however, *almost* the same, yet slightly—disturbingly—out of tune. The fact is, octaves and fifths, when created with Pythagoras's pure mathematical ratios, are incommensurate: The further they move away from a common starting point, the more the structures built from these "perfect" intervals diverge. Like "unutterable" numbers, they defy all efforts at containment.

There is a contemporary mathematical explanation of why a series of fifths starting out from *do* will never complete a perfect circle (by eventually arriving at another harmonious

Boethius playing a monochord and Pythagoras testing different-sized bells (top panels), from a twelfth-century manuscript

do) but will instead reach toward infinity in an unending spiral. It goes as follows: Octaves are based on multiples of *two* (they are formed by the proportion 2:1) and fifths are based on multiples of *three* (they are formed by the proportion 3:2). Both two and three are *prime* numbers, numbers that have as their factors only themselves and the number one. And powers of *different* prime numbers can never be equal, no matter how many times you multiply them. Picture two carpenters installing bookshelves together in someone's home, each using one of these scales of measurement. Carpenter number one uses octaves as his measure; carpenter number two uses fifths. Their brackets will never align to form an even plane.

After beginning their journey together on a particular note, the series of octaves and the series of fifths can *never* again meet at exactly the same place. Their differing scales of measurement won't allow it. Faced with this problem, Pythagoras simply left well enough alone: Music of his time was not seriously affected by the discrepancy. Infused with poetic rhythm, clinging to the inflections of speech, and soaked in the colors of the East, Greek song bore none of the complex harmonies or wide-ranging musical patterns that would expose the mismatched concordances, and so they would not require attention—for the time being. Like occupants of a magnificent Trojan horse, the secret cracks in Pythagoras's laws of proportion would lie in wait. Their moment would come.

4

So Many Bells

But oh! what art can teach,
What human voice can reach
         The sacred organ's praise?
    Notes inspiring holy love,
Notes that wing their heavenly ways
    To mend the choirs above.

—John Dryden, "A Song for Saint Cecilia's Day"

Winchester cathedral shuddered and roared as seventy men, dripping with sweat and urging each other on, pumped in unison to force air through four hundred magnificent vibrating pipes. As the thunderous sound echoed throughout the stately chapel and beyond, Wulfstan the cantor placed his palms over his ears to blot out the clamor. The organ tones were loud—so loud they could be heard throughout the city. And as the tenth century drew to a close, reports of the marvelous noise of Winchester cathedral spread across England.

At least, so wrote the good cantor in a poem of praise to

his mighty instrument. Centuries after the dissolution of the great Greek empire, music continued to enthrall. Indeed, Wulfstan and his ilk marveled at the organ's ability to shepherd the souls of listeners; the instrument seemed to draw worshipers the way the divine mover impelled the heavenly spheres.

One day such keyboards would be Pythagoras's undoing, but musical art in the time of Wulfstan left the incongruities in his ancient formulas unrevealed. In any case, the power of Winchester's sound had less to do with musical proportion than with rousing, raw sensation. The ghost of Pythagoras continued to loom, nonetheless. It was, after all, his powerful blend of order and wonder that served as a winning model for kings, emperors, and popes—most often, wonder used in service to the reigning order. And man created great organs.

Cicero called its sound as pleasing to the ear as the tastiest fish is to the palate. The emperor Nero bragged that he played one. By the second century, the organ could be heard at games, circuses, and gladiator contests. As the Middle Ages wore on, it grew from a pleasing diversion to a political tool of considerable value. In 757 the emperor Constantine Copronymus sent an organ to Pepin, king of the Franks. The king of Constantinople had one delivered to Charlemagne in 812, complete with bronze pipes, bull-leather bellows, and three sound effects: rumbling thunder, tremulous lyre, and tinkling cymbals. Charlemagne ordered it studied so he could construct his own, but the undertaking failed.

The Venetian poet Ermoldus Nigellus recorded a rivalry between two great powers. It was settled in 826 by the priest Georgius when he succeeded in building an organ at Aachen for Louis the Pious: "That organ, which France never pro-

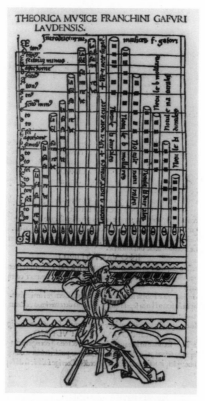

An organ diagram from *Theorica Musicae* by Italian composer Franchino Gafori (1451–1522)

duced—how proudly the Greeks gloried in that fact—and by which Constantinople thought to surpass Thee, oh Emperor: now it stands at the court of Aachen." The showier the organ, the greater the effect. By the thirteenth century, an organ of ninety pipes came to be used as a diplomatic offering from an Arab palace to the emperor of China.

Temperament

Organs were not the only musical machines that could quicken the medieval pulse. In the royal courts, mechanical musicmakers called *automata* were prized; despite their primitive musicality, they too provoked the kind of astonishment that aroused Cantor Wulfstan's poetic sensibilities. The emir of Babylon owned an automaton: a gilded copper tree covered with pneumatically powered singing birds. Visitors at the court of the Great Khan found a silver tree ornamented by lions and serpents that dispensed milk, among other refreshments. At the top was an angel with a movable trumpet, connected by a tube to a man hidden below. When a drink was requested, a shout would go out for the angel to blow his trumpet, and the resulting fanfare signaled the servants to deliver their goods.

The thrill of these spectacles energized artisans throughout Europe. A Strasbourg clock, begun in 1352, contained a carillon that played hymns and was adorned with statues of the Virgin and Child with three Magi, as well as a mechanical rooster that crowed and flapped its wings; it also contained a tablet demonstrating the correlation between the zodiac and the parts of the body, conveniently indicating proper times for bloodletting. Even professional musicians found these devices impressive: The celebrated fourteenth-century composer Guillaume de Machaut was much taken with the "wonders, sports, artifices, machinery, watercourses, entertainments, and strange things" in the collection of Robert of Artois.

Mechanical musicmakers wound their way uneasily into the heart of the church, at first provoking terror as often as awe. Saint Dunstan was accused of sorcery when he produced an Aeolian harp whose strings were set in motion by the air rushing through the cracks in a cathedral wall. What's more, musicmakers were at first seen as an unwelcome diversion from the proper business of religion. Augustine had condemned the frivolous pleasures that distract men from matters of the spirit, noting the church's poor attendance when it faced competition from scantily clad dancing girls; music, he discovered, could also be a troublesome enticement. The venerable sage was so overwhelmed upon hearing the men and women of Milan jointly sing the hymns of Saint Ambrose he wept with joy, but confessed that while listening to music he sometimes found himself moved more by the voices than by the words—beguiled by the sheer pleasure of the sound—and thus became guilty of penal sin. The God of the Bible is a jealous god.

Concern about the use of organs followed similar lines. A warning was issued by Saint Aelred, soon to be abbot of the Cistercian Rievaulx Abbey, in 1141: "Why in the church so many organa, so many bells? For what, I ask, this fearful bellows-blast, more able to express the crash of thunder than the sweetness of the voice? . . . Meanwhile, the people standing, trembling and thunderstruck, wonder at the noise of the bellows, the clashing of bells and the harmony of pipes."

There were reasons for alarm. As the Western Roman Empire struggled against chaos at the end of the fourth century, the Roman Ammianus observed that music had displaced philosophy and turned the libraries into "tombs." Among the culprits cited: gigantic hydraulic organs and lyres as large as chariots. Nevertheless, when faced with the peril of dancing girls, fire must be met with fire. Besides, an age-old doctrine lent weight to the view that organs could actually preserve the church from ruin—as well as increase social order and personal morality.

Once again, the idea came from ancient Greece. Plato (taking a cue from Pythagoras) taught that correct musical proportions reflect the vibrations of man's inner nature, just as they mirror the harmony of the celestial spheres spinning in their orbits. Music, he said, could thus be used to "correct any discord which may have arisen in the courses of the soul." Ominously, the reverse was also possible. The Roman orator Quintilian, a frequently cited authority in the medieval universities, left us to ponder the sad story of a piper accused of manslaughter. He had played a tune to accompany a sacrifice but used the wrong musical scale, "with the result that the person officiating went mad and flung himself over a precipice."

By the second century Clement of Alexandria had succeeded in inserting the image of Christ into this picture: Now it was the Son of God who composed the melodious order of creation, tuning the discords of the elements until the whole universe was in perfect resonance. Consequently, from earliest times, number, sound, and virtue wrapped themselves like intertwining vines around the trunk of Western culture.

It was a compelling tangle. Perhaps Pope John VIII had it in mind as he struggled to shore up his precarious papacy at the end of the ninth century, when he advocated church organs "for the purpose of teaching the science of music." (Anything was worth a try. One-third of the popes elected between 872 and 1012 died through strangulation, suffocation, mutilation, or other violent acts. Unfortunately, John VIII was himself bludgeoned by his own retinue. Even Pythagoras couldn't help.)

There were, of course, those who refused to fall under the master of Croton's spell, even in ancient Greece. Aristoxenus, a student of Aristotle, rejected Pythagoras's musical laws as contrivances—just as the iconoclastic playwright Critias suggested that the gods themselves were merely an invention. Yet the grip of those mystical numbers and stealthy spirits proved unshakable. Plato's pronouncements, echoed by important writers like Cicero, Boethius, and Macrobius, pointed the church toward an ideal music: one made of sounds that would emulate the choirs of heaven.

That sonorous ideal was found not in clangorous bells and ferocious bellows, but in the contemplative strains of devotional melodies called plainchant: simple tunes, incantory and plaintive, buoyed gently on the breaths of choristers. These softly arching communal prayers drifted through a church chamber like clouds of incense—more ritual than performance, the music of surrender.

Chant was prized for its guileless simplicity and rendered at first as a solitary, unadorned tune. Its purity was bound to fall prey to human ambition. This music began to change as singers learned to intone Pythagoras's perfect fifths or perfect fourths above the original line to create a sound called organum. The effect was hollow and haunting—slowly shifting pillars of sound perfectly suited to resonant high cathedral walls. But it was only the beginning.

Artfully executed organum quickly became a source of pride. Bored monks in search of amusement began to invent and collect variations; embellishment crept in to impose its own crafty influence. What had been singing of faceless obeisance slowly took on the luster of display—the vocal equivalent to crashing cymbals and rumbling pipes. The music was no longer merely a dutiful expression of the transcendent but something alluring; it had become an object of desire.

The impulse to explore greater musical horizons demanded advances in technology. In the eleventh century, Guido of Arezzo, a monk of Pomposa, introduced an important one. He gave names to the notes of the musical scale—by taking the first syllables of each half-line of a hymn to John the Baptist—and created a musical staff on which to notate them. (The lines "Ut queant laxis resonare floris" yielded *ut* [today we use *do*] and *re*; "Mira gestorum famuli tuorum" gave us *mi* and *fa*; "Solve polluti labii reatum" resulted in *sol* and *la*.) A new literacy illuminated the musical landscape. Portraying music visually made its structures easier to grasp and to vary; it enabled choirboys to learn in a few days what had taken weeks, and gave singers and composers newfound freedom to experiment. Musicians could more easily pose the question: What if . . . ?

What if singers broke away from traditional tunes, allowing their voices to dance and weave at will? What if different voices singing at the same time each followed their own rhythms? What if the old forms were to dissolve, giving birth to an entirely new sound?

As early as 1132 a statute of the Cistercian Order attempted to combat the change. Men, it complained, should cease singing "in a womanish manner with tinkling . . . as if imitating the wantonness of minstrels." Nevertheless, the spirit of adventure prevailed. By 1324 the sins of virtuosity had grown so great they provoked the first papal bull devoted entirely to music. Innovating composers, bemoaned Pope John XXII, would now habitually "chop up the melodies . . .

so that these rush around ceaselessly, intoxicating the ear without quieting it, and disturbing devotion instead of evoking it." The pontiff was especially offended by a rhythmic device known as *hocket* (from the Latin and French for "hiccup"), employing short, rapid exchanges between voices. The music of the divine offices was "pestered" with these short notes, he announced, and "depraved" with secular melodies so that "wantonness, which ought to be eschewed, increases." The pope, whose good offices were also being pestered at the time by an epidemic of clergy charged with practicing sorcery, demanded a return to simple parallel organum. "Music was originally discreet, seemly, simple, masculine, and of good morals," agreed Jacques de Liège, author of the most extensive extant medieval treatise on music; "have not the moderns rendered it lascivious beyond measure?"

By that time, musical compositions had indeed become wildly elaborate, overtaking by leaps and bounds the sense of play that musical ingenuity had fostered early on. In the thirteenth century, for example, a piece was written in which the chant melody reversed itself and ran backward—the word *Dominus* now rendered as *Nusmido*. By the fourteenth century, multilingual compositions called motets (written for many individual strands of voices) had brought such quaint practices to staggering heights. The motet *Dieus! comment porrai laisser la vie/O regina gloriae* was but one example: The bottom part consisted of a chant melody; the middle, a glorification of the Virgin Mary: "O queen of glory, hope of the faithful, hear the prayer of the supplicants of your confraternity." Meanwhile, the upper part, as if operating in another time and place, casually vocalized: "God! How could I leave life in Paris with my comrades? Never for good, they are so delightful. For when they are all gathered together, each one sets himself to laugh and play and sing."

Music's more intricate textures, requiring new levels of precision and coordination, had been encouraged by the measured pulse of the mechanical clock, and influenced by advances in mathematics such as the introduction of Arabic numerals and the sign for zero. Mathematicians, in turn, were spurred on by musicians. The mathematician and astronomer Levi ben Gerson wrote his treatise *De harmonicis numeris* at the urging of composer Philippe de Vitry (who was also an advisor to the kings of France, a diplomat at the papal court, and, eventually, bishop of Meaux). Nicholas Oresme, perhaps the most influential genius of the Middle Ages in economics, mathematics, and science, dedicated his treatise *Algorismus proportionum* to Philippe, "whom I would call Pythagoras if it were possible to believe in the opinion about the return of souls."

In addition to the deft cerebrations of these thinkers, another, more earthy influence was also at work. In time it would pervade all of the arts, though its impact was felt strongly and early on in the paintings of a single Florentine artist. His name was Giotto, described by the celebrated writer Boccaccio as the ugliest-looking man in Italy. In *The Divine Comedy*, however, Dante proclaimed Giotto the supreme purveyor of artistic beauty. Leonardo da Vinci would one day announce: "After him art declined."

His painterly revolution was based on a simple principle: Giotto breathed into his subjects a spirit of life that previous painters had denied them. The artist cast aside the tone of philosophical remove invoked by his contemporaries: In his hands, rigid forms relaxed into natural postures and familiar landscapes; expressionless faces melted into the agonies and joys of a fleshly existence. He placed people in the lower half of a picture, so that instead of having to peer up at them, viewers would be drawn into the scene. Studying Giotto's frescoes in 1874, the English critic John Ruskin commented, "He painted the Madonna and St. Joseph and the Christ— yes, by all means, if you choose to call them so—but essentially, Mamma, Papa, and the Baby." Here, suddenly, was the veneration of the purely human.

The new style caused a commotion. Italy's esteemed poet Petrarch—who knew and apparently respected Giotto— nevertheless complained of "images bursting from their frames, and the lineaments of breathing faces, so that you expect shortly to hear the sound of their voices. It is here in that the danger lies, for great minds are greatly taken with this."

Clearly, even less-than-great minds were taken with it— or with something close to it. Giotto lived until 1337. By 1350, after centuries of unchanging costumes in Europe—long tunics that extended to the feet for women and to the knees for men—fashion changed abruptly; men's outfits became shorter and women began wearing closer-fitting dresses, cut with a large décolletage. In Guillaume de Nangis's chronicle, there is an entry reporting "tunics so short and tight that they revealed what modesty bids us hide." Things would never again be the same.

Meanwhile, in music, important composers were increasingly devoting their energies to displaying the lineaments of the body politic. They showed off their new rhythmic sophistication in works like the *Roman de Fauvel,* a satire on social corruption with a story built around an ass (or horse) named Fauvel, whose name derives from the initial letters of several all-too-familiar human characteristics: *flaterie, avarice, vilanie* (baseness), *variété* (inconstancy), *envie,* and *lascheté* (cowardice). (Neither the follies nor the satire ever grew out of date; from the expression "to curry Fauvel" we still happily use the phrase "to curry favor.")

Politics proved a fertile ground for musical creation. When the most powerful institution in the world was split asunder in 1378 with the election of two competing popes, musicians were at the ready. The great schism led to even greater social discontent and increasing nationalist fervor; it also doubled the opportunities for musical ceremony. Thus, when the besieged Roman Pope Urban VI fled from Naples to a castle in Nocernia in 1385, he was able to enjoy a freshly composed motet that included a recitation of his troubles, written to console him. (According to reports, he listened contentedly while the cries of his tortured prisoners reverberated throughout the castle's corridors.) In an attempt to preserve order, the Parisian police in 1395 forbade all minstrels to make mention of the unity (or disunity) of the church in their songs. The popes, of course, were free to do as they liked.

All this while, keyboards were continuing to develop. The first hints of a new type of instrument come from a letter written by King John I of Aragon, written in 1367. In it, he asks his ambassadors to find someone who can play an instrument "similar to the organ but sounded by means of strings."

Another letter, written in 1397, finds the Paduan lawyer Giovanni Lambertacci informing his son-in-law, a student at the university in Pavia, that his Viennese friend Dr. Hermannus Poll had invented an instrument called the clavicembalum. This intriguing event would impact musical life for centuries to come; unfortunately, Poll would not live to witness it. In what seemed at the time a bit of good luck, the doctor managed to find employment in 1400 as physician to the new German king, Ruprecht of the palatinate; but in 1401 his careers in both music and medicine were abruptly ended as a result of his execution in Nuremberg. It appears Poll had plotted to poison the monarch, or so it was alleged—a misfortune for both the good doctor and his many friends, who were left to lament the passing of "an outstanding physician, handsome, well-mannered, 31-year-old master of arts, very literate and a doctor of medicine, an excellent musician on the organ and other musical instruments." Though, it would seem, he was a less-than-skillful politician.

The clavicembalum remains with us today as the harpsichord, a keyboard instrument whose strings are plucked with a quill as the keys are pressed. Although the twentieth-century English conductor Sir Thomas Beecham once described the harpsichord's thin, nasal sound as like that of two skeletons copulating on a tin roof, at the turn of the fifteenth century its creation marked the beginning of a bright new era for instrumental music. Throughout the developments of the Middle Ages, the organ had played a subsidiary role. Now, keyboards of all sorts would begin to assume a more prominent—and problematic—position. Coupled with an increasing desire for new harmonic colors, they would help build a sound world previously unimagined.

A hint of things to come was already in the air: a musical harmony as powerfully transformative as Giotto's frescoes.

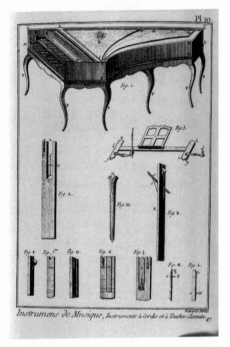

A harpsichord and its jacks, from Denis Diderot and Jean Le Rond d'Alembert, *Art du faiseur d'instruments de musique et lutherie* (Paris, 1785)

This combination of tones, which we call *thirds,* fell outside the acceptable Pythagorean canon of octaves, fifths, and fourths. It had already been present in some musical works, but only as fleeting collisions of independent melodies. Now it was heard in purposeful, sonorous blocks, at first mostly in the works of English composers. By the fifteenth century, however, it would be in use throughout the Continent. In some deep, inscrutable way, this sumptuous harmony imbued music with a more human face.

Around 1355, the Dutch priest and music theorist Johannes Boen, envisioning a future of new instruments and heightened musical skills, predicted that "many new and unheard-of things will arise . . . with the passing of time." Now, the world he dreamed of was just around the corner.

5

The Search for *La:*
A Musical Puzzle

A god has power. But can a mere man follow
The lyre's subtle music? Out of joint
His senses are. And at the crossing point
Of heart-ways stands no Temple of Apollo.

—Rainer Maria Rilke, "The Poet"

The early, primitive keyboard was not very useful for showcasing a performer's technical prowess—that is, unless the performer was Francesco Landini, Italy's foremost fourteenth-century musician. Though blinded in childhood by smallpox, Landini rose to the highest ranks as a poet, composer, organ builder—and keyboard virtuoso. The Florentine chronicler Filippo Villani reported that Landini played "as readily as though he had the use of his eyes, with a touch of such rapidity (yet always observing the measure), with such skill and sweetness that beyond all doubt he excelled beyond comparison all organists who can possibly be remembered."

In Giovanni da Prato's *Paradiso degli Alberti* (in which he depicted events of the year 1389—or claimed to), Landini appears as a kind of musical sorcerer: "Now the sun rose higher and the heat of the day increased," wrote da Prato,

> and the whole company remained in the pleasant shade; and as a thousand birds were singing among the verdant branches, someone asked Francesco to play the organ a little, to see whether the sound would make the birds increase or diminish their song. He did so at once, and a great wonder followed: for when the sound began many of the birds were seen to fall silent, and gather around as if in amazement, listening for a long time; and then they resumed their song and redoubled it, showing inconceivable delight, and especially one nightingale, who came and perched above the organ on a branch over Francesco's head.

The organist's talent was apparently so overwhelming it could win the admiration of a nightingale. Or perhaps his renderings verged so close to the sounds of nature that even the birds were fooled. Landini's work was, after all, touched by the same striving for earthy sensuality that had invaded painting and literature. (It might have been pedigree; Landini's father, the artist Jacopo del Casentino, was a follower of Giotto and a co-founder of the Florentine guild of painters.) Landini's lyrical, florid melodies were often supported by harmonic textures of uncommon lushness.

The English had long since assimilated these harmonies

into a national style. By the late fifteenth century, music theorist Johannes Tinctoris would point to them in summing up the musical art that had blossomed in his lifetime as one "whose fount and origin is held to be among the English, of whom [composer John] Dunstable stood forth as chief." Of course, never one to give credit easily, Tinctoris also managed to include in his observations the fact that the English "shout"—unlike the French, who "sing"—and that they had come to rely on too much of a good thing, or, to put it less kindly (as he did), that they demonstrate "a wretched poverty of invention."

Regional differences had always had a hand in shaping musical character. Charlemagne learned this lesson when he attempted to install plainchant in all the lands under his control. In Italy, singers obliged easily, he discovered, but those living further north were another story: They had "coarse voices, which roar like thunder," reported John the Deacon, and couldn't sing the delicate melodies of chant "because their throats are hoarse with too much drinking." Over time, the tender Italians had transformed those melodies into the complex art of an age. Now, as Europe lurched toward a great renaissance, it was England's turn to exert a tug on the musical compass.

The new "English" harmonies were called thirds. We can find thirds on our keyboard by beginning once again with *do*.

The musical stretch, or interval, from *do* to *mi* (or from *fa* to *la* or *sol* to *ti*) is a *major third*. It results from having two tones vibrating in the proportion 5:4. Sung from the top note down to the bottom one, this interval was used by Beethoven for the famous opening thunderbolts of his Fifth Symphony:

The Search for *La:* A Musical Puzzle

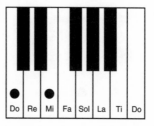

mi-mi-mi do! The folk song "Kumbaya" outlines this third in its first two rising notes.

The sound of this harmony is sweet and liquid; not airy like a fifth (*do* to *sol*), but more condensed, tantalizingly palpable. If the open harmony of a fifth symbolically bridges the dust of the earth and the ceiling of heaven, the sound of a third fills that chasm with something warm and delicious: in a way, the song of the human heart.

There are actually two kinds of thirds. The span of a *minor third*—formed by the proportion 6:5—can be found between *re* and *fa,* or between *mi* and *sol.* The distance between its two notes is shorter than that of a major third by one *half-step*—the smallest distance between any two notes on the keyboard. If we were to equate sounds with colors, the minor third would be darker and deeper than the major third. It is associated in romantic musical works with feelings of melancholy or passion; today, it is a mainstay of the blues. Chopin's achingly sad funeral march in his Sonata in B-flat minor is launched (after four repetitions of its first note) with the leap of a minor third.

As far back as the thirteenth century, the English had demonstrated a predilection for thirds, and for their mirror images—sixths. (To find a sixth, raise that low *do* so that it is

Temperament

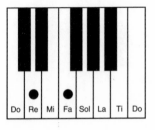

now above *mi*—the result is a sixth rather than a third.) Though they were not considered concords in Pythagorean musical practice, one English commentator (known as Anonymous IV), writing around 1280, described these harmonies as the most agreeable of all. They first arose not in the work of theorists, but through a dynamic folk tradition: People liked these sounds. According to one observer, the more they were used by singing voices, the merrier the result.

Thirds made their way into some of the earliest music written for organ. A fourteenth-century collection called the Robertsbridge Manuscript includes pieces in which a series of thirds move in parallel motion (like graceful deer running in formation), which is just the way they were used in singing. The fifteenth-century German organist Conrad Paumann (another blind musician of uncommon talent) took up the practice, and used thirds and fifths simultaneously in his organ works, forming full-textured musical harmonies called *triads* (or three-note *chords*)—the foundation for music's next stylistic era.

Using these sounds on mechanical instruments—which were now expanding in size and range—was a natural development. But it marked a turning point: the historical moment when an infamous musical paradox began to cause musicians serious practical problems.

To understand why, let's construct a virtual keyboard. The first step is to gather all the parts: wood for the keys and frame; quills to pluck the strings; and, of course, the strings themselves—in many different lengths. Each length will vibrate at its own particular frequency; the longer the string, the lower its tone.

We'll begin by selecting a string of medium length and installing it for the key we call *do.* (Today, there is a standard length for *do;* but we are constructing our instrument during the Middle Ages.)

To find the correct string lengths for the rest of the keyboard's notes we'll apply the proportions we learned from Pythagoras. For *sol,* a perfect fifth above, we will select a shorter string to form the ratio 3:2 with *do.* Our *sol* string (assuming, again, that tension and materials are consistent) will thus be two-thirds the length of the string for *do.*

We can select the string for *fa* by using the formula for a perfect fourth above *do.* The proportion between the string length for *do* and the one for *fa* will be 4:3.

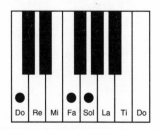

Next, we'll find the proper string for *re* by calculating a perfect fourth below *sol.* Once again, the proportion between those two strings will be 4:3, with the lower tone getting the longer string.

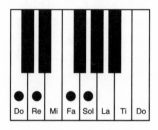

So far, all has gone smoothly. As we continue, searching next for the correct string length of *la*, however, difficulties abound. There is more than one option. For example, *la* lies a perfect fifth above *re*, and these two string lengths should form the proportion 3:2. However, *la* could also be a major third above *fa*, so we might form this tone by putting *those* strings in the proportion 5:4. The problem is, the two solutions to finding *la* actually yield different tones. Which one is the real *la*?

The question is crucial. The interval between *fa* and *la* created by means of *Pythagorean* tuning—that is, through a series of perfect fifths (3:2)—will be slightly wider than the "pure" third (5:4) the human ear finds so rich and re-warding; as a result, its sound is far less pleasant—edgy, even acidic. But the *la* that is a pure, lovely major third above *fa* is unacceptably ugly when serving in harmony as the fifth of *re*.

The difference between these two versions of *la* is called a *comma* (in this case, it is known as the comma of Didymus, named after the ancient Greek who first described it, or the *syntonic comma*). In the grammar of languages, a comma provides a pause—the space of a hair's breadth within a sentence. In music, the term also describes a tiny gap, the difference between tones that are so close they share the same name but have been calculated through different proportions. Just as a misplaced comma in the written word has the power to stop a sentence dead in its tracks, an errant musical comma can bring a lyrical cadence to a screeching halt. Indeed, in music, even a numerically infinitesimal gap can seem the sonic equivalent of a harrowing abyss.

Thirds are not the only "problem" interval for keyboards. As we have seen, Pythagoras at his monochord had realized millennia ago the imperfection in his chain of perfect fifths—that in order for the twelve pitches generated through the proportion 3:2 to complete a path from *do* to *do,* the circle has somehow to be adjusted, "rounded off." That is, one "link" in this chain must be made shorter (by a gap known as the Pythagorean comma) so that the top note of the series can form a perfect octave with its lower namesake. But the act of artificially forcing the fifths into a seamless circle dooms that shortened link to an unsavory role. The notes that comprise it create a distorted howling "wolf," to be avoided at all times.

As a result, tuning all the relationships between a keyboard's tones using perfect fifths as the measure simply won't work. However, choosing our keyboard's string lengths by using the formula for pure thirds—5:4—will bring equally disastrous consequences. Three major thirds should theoretically add up to the interval of an octave.

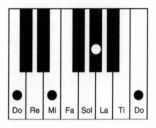

But they don't. Stack three *pure* major thirds, each produced through the proportion 5:4, against a perfect octave, and their resulting span will fall short. Our two carpenters would have an impossible time constructing usable bookshelves if one used thirds as a measure, and the other octaves.

In similar fashion, four minor thirds, built through the proportion 6:5, seem to add up to an octave if we use the keyboard as a guide.

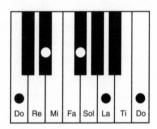

But in reality they produce a span that sounds wider than a pure octave.

As a result, an instrument tuned to preserve perfect fifths can't render the sweetness of pure thirds or sixths. And tuned to preserve pure thirds, it won't produce perfect octaves or perfect fifths. Attempting to force them all into the same harpsichord or organ would be like trying to squeeze various pieces of fine furniture into a room too small to accommodate them; no matter where you place the exquisite couch, there is simply no room for the elegant loveseat. We can achieve gorgeous concordances between certain tones (find room for the couch), but in the process we will guarantee witheringly ugly results between others (mangle the loveseat while trying to force it in). The keyboard thus became a battleground of warring proportions; and the desire to achieve a tuning based on all of the ideal, simple ratios an unrealizable fantasy.

In dealing with this complex situation, musicians were on their own to achieve a workable compromise. Theorists had not yet joined the fracas. The dilemma was, of course, unavoidable—a result of both musical evolution and technological advance. Indeed, even more daring changes were soon to sweep across Europe.

During the period of the church's great schism, a network of long-distance trade had begun to grow, especially through the merchant classes of Italy and Flanders. The world had grown smaller, and musical artists were now sought-after commodities. Powerful secular courts helped developments along, answering the inherent conservatism of the church with lavish celebrations of the new.

Meanwhile, the holy wars were finally reaching a conclusion. After the Council of Pisa tried unsuccessfully to install yet a third pope in 1409, the Council of Constance was initiated in 1414 to bring an end to disunity, and in 1417 it produced a new leader, Pope Martin V. This time, the resolution held. Musicians from all parts of Europe joined in a colossal celebration, and Rome became the center of sacred music for the next two centuries.

It was around this time that England's most influential composer, John Dunstable, accompanied the Duke of Bedford to France. Bedford commanded the English armies in their fight against Joan of Arc. Dunstable brought along his full-textured approach to composition, characterized by a pervasive sweetness, an avoidance of harsh dissonance, and a freer use of thirds and sixths. (The fields of war are often fertile grounds for musical innovation. As countries ambitiously extend their reach, composers and performers expand their art. The wars of the Renaissance and the conflicts arising over keyboard tunings were, in some ways, related battles.)

The impact of Dunstable's style would prove considerable. Although the use of thirds will continue to serve for a while merely as attractive new flavors in an old stew, their influence will shape everything to come.

6

Frozen Music

Heard melodies are sweet, but those unheard
Are sweeter; therefore, ye soft pipes, play on;
Not to the sensual ear, but, more endeared,
Pipe to the spirit ditties of no tone . . .

—John Keats, "Ode on a Grecian Urn"

The new music flourished in the courts of Burgundy under the dukes of the house of Valois, a reign that began with a grant of land by King Charles V to Philip the Bold in the mid–fourteenth century. Through marriage and uncommon political skill, Philip and his successors—John the Fearless, Philip the Good, and Charles the Bold—managed not only to keep control of the region of northeastern France with Dijon as its capital, but to add to their domain such valuable assets as Flanders, Holland, and a patchwork of other territories. By the early fifteenth century, Burgundy had become the most influential spot in Western Europe, its dukes the equal of kings.

Artistic splendor became the courtly face of political

ambition. Talented instrumentalists were imported from France, England, Italy, Germany, Portugal, Sicily, and else-where. Musical patronage was exercised so grandly that the period is now known as "the Burgundian epoch," and the music of the time, the "Burgundian school." The court's great chapel boasted unparalleled musical forces. Separate bands of minstrels were kept on hand for secular celebra-tions, like the banquet thrown midcentury by Philip the Good in which revelers, drinking wine from flowing foun-tains, observed allegorical tableaux of ancient adventures—Jason searching for the Golden Fleece, or Mother Church, dressed in black, mourning the fall of Constantinople from atop an elephant. (European pageantry had enjoyed the pres-ence of the great gray mammoth as far back as Charle-magne, who owned one named Abu-Lubabah, or "the Father of Intelligence." A gift from the sultan Haroun-al-Raschid, the creature accompanied the emperor throughout his trav-els, until its demise during a campaign against the Danes in 810.) Throughout the celebration, an ensemble of twenty-eight musicians performed from within a giant mock pie. One does not live by hymns alone.

Despite such colorful spectacles, however, Burgundy's true legacy is the serious art it produced. Some of the most gifted musicians of the day could be found there. The blind organ virtuoso Conrad Paumann—Germany's leading figure in instrumental music—performed for Philip the Good. Guil-laume Dufay, whose music would profoundly influence nearly every composer of the fifteenth century, was a cele-brated guest.

More than anyone else, Dufay set the course for the musi-cal language of the Renaissance, combining the harmonic richness heard in the music of the English composers (with whom he had contact in the 1420s) with a skillful command of the intricate rhythms and textures found in the music of Northern Europe. The results could be stunning, as in his gorgeous *Ave Regina caelorum,* where the text "have mercy on thy dying Dufay" is poignantly underscored by the dark, dramatic harmonies of minor thirds. The composer stated in his will that this was the work he wished to be sung as he was drawing his last breaths.

Those rich, sensuous thirds played an increasingly important part in the new musical order, but Pythagoras's ratios had not completely ceded their supremacy. In fact, they permeate one of Dufay's most famous pieces, written for the dedication of Filippo Brunelleschi's new dome crowning the Florence cathedral known as Santa Maria del Fiore. Dufay was in Florence as a singer in the papal choir when he received the commission from Pope Eugenius IV, who had settled there while escaping his enemies in Rome. This church holds a special place in Florence's history.

Before the construction of its dome, Santa Maria del Fiore had sat for half a century without a crown. Completing the structure—which required the placement of a vault across a 138-foot span—had seemed an impossible feat. By Dufay's time desperation for a solution had set in, prompting wildly impractical suggestions. One was to pack the church with a mixture of earth and coins; workers would climb atop this homemade mountain to complete the roof. Then, after the dome was set above this solid floor, went the idea, the soil would be removed by Florentine children eager to carry it off, sift through the grains, and recover the hidden money.

Eventually, a contest was held in search of a practical

answer. Brunelleschi had already engaged in a competition for the design of the north doors of the Florence baptistery; however, the commission ultimately went to sculptor Lorenzo Ghiberti. (Michelangelo later declared Ghiberti's doors to be "so fine that they might fittingly stand at the Gates of Paradise.") But Filippo Brunelleschi was not the sort to be easily discouraged. Contemporary accounts paint someone thoroughly convinced of his own abilities—not to say contentious as a mule. He once spent eleven days in jail rather than pay his annual dues to the stonemasons and woodworkers' guild. When the powerful Cosimo de' Medici dared to criticize his model for a proposed palace, he smashed it to pieces. His adopted twenty-two-year-old son fled to Naples with some of Brunelleschi's money, and the architect unhesitatingly petitioned the pope to intervene in the family squabble.

His gifts were undeniable, however, and he knew it. Challenged by Giovanni di Gherardo da Prato to an exchange of insulting sonnets ("Oh you deep fountain, pit of igno-rance, / You miserable beast and imbecile. . . . / There is no substance to your alchemy. . . . / Surely you are mad," went the opening flurry), Brunelleschi was self-assured and glib: "For wise men nothing that exists / Remains unseen . . . / Only the artist, not the fool, / Discovers that which nature hides."

He was confident of discovering the thus-far hidden solu-tion to the problem of constructing the church dome, and set out with his friend and fellow artist Donatello to hunt for it among the artifacts of Rome. The veneration of classical antiquity had been a cultural trend since 1402, when the Flo-rentines, proud of their success at foiling the attempted conquest of Tuscany by the Duke of Milan, recalled a similar defeat of the Persians at the hands of the Athenians and began to think of themselves as citizens of a "new Athens." No battle had decided the outcome for Florence: The siege simply failed of its own inertia after their foe contracted a fever and died. Nevertheless, in the euphoria of the moment, and with pride in their increasing wealth and artistry, the inhabitants of Florence adopted the "Athens" label. From the start of the fifteenth century, a flurry of translations of manuscripts from the ancient world added fuel to these fires.

While in Rome, Brunelleschi and his companion became especially intrigued by the Pantheon—a majestic structure built in 125 C.E., and capped by a huge dome. Leon Battista Alberti, who, after Brunelleschi, occupied a prime position among Italy's artists, pointed to the Pantheon in his treatise on architecture as a model for all holy spaces, its design a visible embodiment of "divine proportion."

The Pantheon is calculated to inspire such feelings. There is a palpable geometry to its interior space. The reach from its floor to its summit is exactly the length of its diameter—144 feet—creating a frame of two large intersecting circles, like the outlines of an imaginary globe. Coffers arranged in horizontal bands along the lower curves of the ceiling seem almost to swirl as their rows rise upward, away from the convex floor below. The dome, a concrete shell, was secretly constructed in two layers in order to support its enormous weight; a dramatic thirty-foot circular hole at the dome's center is the building's only source of light.

Brunelleschi searched, studied, measured, and returned with a plan. He proposed two thin shells for the Florence dome, one inside and one out. And, in a remarkable stroke of imagination, he suggested a way of building the giant cupola without the benefit of "centering"—the traditional method requiring structural scaffolding. (It was just one in a stream of Brunelleschi's radical ideas, which also included machines for lifting weights to the top of a construction site, and a way to mechanically propel a boat.) To support the dome, he recommended a skeleton of twenty-four ribs, anchored at the top by a heavy lantern to counterbalance their natural tendency to tilt outward from the center.

Critics doubted his ability to pull it off. The Florentine authorities, hoping for the best possible result, tried to engineer a collaboration between Ghiberti and his former competitor; but both the concept and credit for its eventual completion belong to Brunelleschi.

He received approval to begin in 1420. Workers labored fifteen years before the dome rose majestically "above the skies, ample to cover with its shadow all the Tuscan people," in the words of Alberti. It was a magnificent achievement, matched by Dufay's musical tribute, the motet *Nuper rosarum flores.* An eyewitness to the dedication, at which the pope himself officiated, wrote of the bright-robed instrumentalists and choristers, the sound of the music, and the perfume of incense. The overall effect was "as though the symphonies and songs of the angels and of divine paradise had been sent forth from Heaven to whisper in our ears an unbelievable celestial sweetness. Wherefore in that moment I was so possessed by ecstasy," wrote our reporter, "that I seemed to enjoy the life of the blessed here on earth." Also ecstatic were the fourteen condemned prisoners released to the pope as a benevolent gesture in honor of the occasion.

Frozen Music

Dufay's music was equal to the occasion, though celebrants, swept away by what their eyes and ears perceived, might not have noticed the subtle connection between the church building and the sounds used to commemorate it. Nevertheless, evidence suggests that the composer of *Nuper rosarum flores* had not merely written a beautiful piece, but had carefully calibrated the structure of his work to correspond to certain ancient proportions, used for centuries specifically for the construction of sacred spaces.

For Dufay, as for many composers before him, music was, in Leonardo da Vinci's phrase, "the shaping of the invisible." His approach to the motet *Nuper rosarum flores* sprang from a medieval musical tradition grounded in concealed meanings. Composers often disguised liturgical melodies by stretching them beyond recognition, or shaped their musical forms through secret rhythmic patterns. Art thus hatched bespoke their view of the world as a place filled with puzzlement. Where does fire go when it's put out? How can the earth, with its tremendous heft, remain suspended in thin air? Though faith left no doubt of a divine purpose behind it all, life's fabric was nevertheless embedded with riddles, and medieval musicians used their art to imitate this state of affairs. They crafted works on a foundation of veiled principles, or seeded them with cryptic signs, so that beneath the surface of sound an imperceptible force of reason was always at work.

It was not extraordinary, then, for Dufay to etch his music around a symbolic shape. The rarity was that in *Nuper rosarum flores* he appears to have used the proportions of a temple as his template, and not just any temple, but the paradigm of all sacred spaces: the Temple of Solomon. To design the rhythmic proportions of his piece, Dufay reached deep into the well of architecture's mystic tradition.

The medieval idea of beauty as *splendor veritatis*—the radiance of truth—exerted its influence nowhere more than in the art of church building. God was, after all, the Master Builder, hence churches were required to be more than mere shrines: They became models of the celestial abode toward which each soul should strive. Saint Augustine even set ground rules for their construction, prescribing the proper physical proportions to be used. The heights, lengths, and depths of these structures were to form the proportions 1:1, 1:2, 2:3, and 3:4—Pythagoras's celestial harmonies, now frozen into concrete form.

Religious commentators after Augustine built on this foundation through a combination of biblical interpretation and Platonic mysticism. Thus, by the twelfth century we find the influential philosopher-monk Peter Abelard citing the dimensions of Solomon's Temple as proof of God's desire to materialize his sanctuaries out of a musical harmony. The proportions of that temple—formed by comparing its total length, the length of its house of prayer and of the inner sanctum where the priests performed their mysteries, and of its height—were the very ratios used by Dufay to regulate the rhythms of his piece. The duration of the notes used in the work's rhythms, which change from one section to another, form the ratios of Solomon's Temple: 6:4:2:3. (The lengths used for these calculations were derived from biblical passages in I Kings 6. Of course, *differing* accounts of Solomon's Temple may be found in II Chronicles and in

Ezekiel. But why further muddle an idea that was so awfully complicated to begin with?)

A similar metaphysical geometry permeated the designs of Gothic cathedrals from Abelard's time onward, bringing a special grace to the façade of Notre-Dame in Paris, for example, through a special sequence of squares; and to the interior of the cathedral at Reims, where a series of equilateral triangles is traced by the ribs under its vault. Through divinely inspired number and shape, these churches were transformed from mere buildings into sermons in stone. Dufay's musical use of this architectural numerology was a tribute not only to the great dome in Florence, but to the entire church-building tradition in which his compatriot Brunelleschi labored.

Yet, changes to that tradition were already afoot, led in great part by Brunelleschi himself. The arrival of thirds in music raised questions about the inevitability of the ancient proportions; now, developments in the other arts were about to do the same. Brunelleschi's flights of imagination, his unique and often daring solutions, his willingness to break from accepted modes of thought in order to adapt to the challenges of the moment—all signaled a shift toward an art informed by *experience* as well as by doctrine.

The dream of eternal beauty through a perfect harmony of parts continued to motivate artists of every stripe. Yet the desire to invest painting and sculpture with a greater sense of the real was also now growing in leaps and bounds. Brunelleschi's greatest contribution to this effort was his success in achieving a startling effect: the projection of three-dimensional space on a flat surface. For the rest of the century, artists would follow his lead, attempting to broker a compromise between two points of view: the ancient one, from the distant perch of heaven, where the cosmos assembles itself into abstract, immutable forms; and the newer, through the lens of an eye, where images of the world stream across a filter of human limitation and longing.

Brunelleschi first demonstrated the power of that filter in his dramatic painting of the church of San Giovanni, also know as the Florence Baptistery. Colleagues were astounded by the realism he achieved. The artist began with a small panel, on which he portrayed as much of San Giovanni as could be seen from a fixed position within the central portal of the church of Santa Maria del Fiore, which stood opposite. That is, he set out to paint the church not in an ideal form, but as an object caught from a particular *perspective,* as if observed through (as Alberti would later put it) a window looking out into a section of the world. Brunelleschi's window was, by its nature, a funnel of subjectivity, and this was the secret of his success. Using a narrow perceptual frame—skewing the proportions of the scene to accommodate a particular point of view—allowed him to create a painting of unrivaled realism.

According to his contemporary and biographer Antonio Manetti, Brunelleschi drew San Giovanni with "such care and delicacy and with such great precision . . . that no miniaturist could have done it better." Then he placed burnished silver where the sky would be. Next he put a hole "the size of a lentil bean" through the painting. Viewers were invited to position themselves outdoors, in front of the church, and to place their eye against the hole in the back of the painting. As they peered through the hole directly into a mirror held opposite the painting's front, the image they saw was so compellingly lifelike they doubted it was not the actual church. (The blue of the sky above, along with its drifting clouds, washed across the painting's silver trim, so that nature herself lent power to the scene.)

There was a trick behind it all: The viewing hole was situated at a spot artists now recognize as the "vanishing point"—the site in a painting where receding parallel lines beginning at the front (the part "closest" to the viewer) appear to converge as the picture moves into the "distance." By learning to locate this point precisely, painters ever after have gained the marvelous ability to beguile the eye with illusory depth. Like Giotto before him, Brunelleschi had elevated human sensibility over rigid dogma; in the process he changed painting forever.

The idea of fashioning beauty through a perfect harmony of parts still had vitality. Leon Battista Alberti (who had also arrived in Florence with the pope's suite) was the first painter actually to articulate an explicit technique for achieving perspective in painting, and along the way he recommended that artists study the rules of music, because "the same numbers that please the ears also fill the eyes and the soul with pleasure." Yet, the human condition—with its fleeting, earthbound grasp of life's rhythms and forms—generated its own, special demands, not always in accord with metaphysical ideals. Artists could no longer rest on invariable rules, or remain impervious to life's ambiguity or haphazard circumstance. Proportion in painting would begin more fully to incorporate physical truth—the way the world looks through a portal, or when spied from around a distant corner—as judged through sensory experience.

Temperament

At this historical moment, in both the visual arts and in music, the tension between abstract principles and sensual reality became a driving force for change. The search for a balance between beauty and truth was at a crossroads.

7

The Harmony of Heaven and Earth

Nature is a temple whose living colonnades
Breathe forth a mystic speech in fitful sighs . . .

—Charles Baudelaire, "Correspondences"

It took more than thirty years following the musical celebration of Brunelleschi's dome before its lantern, finally fitted atop, completed the project. The architect had not lived to see its conclusion. Nevertheless, his monument to artistic ingenuity continued to cast its great shadow over Florence, a city now ever more flush with wealth, and teeming with commerce. Craftsmen and merchants lined the town's streets with endless booths, filling the air with a music of their own—the discordant jabber of bargaining over silks, wools, and fine jewelry. In the marketplace, stone masons and marble workers alone occupied 54 shops; cabinetmakers, 84; the woolen guild, 270. (The gears of trade were often lubricated with a sparkling white wine from San Giovanni which, said one observer, "could wake the dead.") Great art and architecture thrived everywhere, along with a sense of endless possibility.

Into this simmering crucible there arrived a young, talented apprentice artist named Leonardo da Vinci. He was a gifted novice from the countryside, tall and slim, with narrow hips, a broadly framed torso, flowing auburn hair, and, according to his contemporary Paolo Giovio, "the most beautiful face in the world." Vasari claimed that Leonardo's deportment was so gracefully inflected, "he brought refreshment to every downcast spirit." In truth, his own high spirits were often battered by life's lapidary churnings. (A humiliating arrest on charges of homosexuality early in Leonardo's Florentine experience appears to have lingered painfully; years later he confessed to a feeling of revulsion toward the human sexual anatomy.)

As an apprentice in the shop of Florentine artist Andrea del Verrocchio, Leonardo studied the lessons of tradition and soaked in the insights of living masters—men like physician, philosopher, and mathematician Paolo dal Pozzo Toscanelli, who in 1468 had drawn a meridian line along the floor of Santa Maria del Fiore to measure the path of the sun's rays streaming through a hole in the church's ceiling, and thus determine the correct date of Easter. In a famous letter to the Portuguese cleric Fernam Martins, Toscanelli had boldly asserted the viability of reaching the Orient by sailing west, long before others thought it possible. Later, when Columbus peered at the New World rising above the ocean's expanse, Toscanelli's imagined map of the globe was clutched in his hands.

Another important influence was Fazio Cardano, a flamboyant lawyer, physician, and mathematician notorious at the university in Pavia for performing his teaching assignments dressed not in traditional black but in flaming red. Cardano shared the translation he had made of John Peckham's *Perspectiva Communis* with Leonardo; the gift helped set the young artist on his life's path. "Among the studies of natural causes and reasons it is light that most enthralls the observer," wrote Peckham. "Accordingly, perspective should be placed in the forefront of all humane disquisitions and disciplines. . . . In it you will find the glory not only of mathematics but of physics, ornamented with flowers both of the one and of the other." Leonardo's own treatise began where Peckham left off, with the title: "An Introduction to Perspective, that is to say to the Function of the Eye."

Perspective had by now telescoped far beyond the confines of an approach to painting to become the mooring for a whole new philosophy settling over the waters of European culture. *Man* is the measure of all things, it claimed. The idea had, of course, long before been put forward by the ancient sage Protagoras (as Leon Battista Alberti reminded his readers in his treatise on painting). When all is said and done, said Protagoras, *perception* is truth.

His pronouncement became the catchphrase of an age. *Man* is the measure. Humanity's take on the world—however murky, skewed, or whimsical—provided a model as meaningful as any bodiless ideal. Earthly experience now became the engine of progress.

Actually, realistic perspective in painting had existed long before the fifteenth century. The ancient Greeks had used it to breathe remarkable depth and vitality into their art (unlike the Egyptians, who, disinterested in realism, were content to depict people as simple, spiritless forms laid across a flat grid). In fact, Leonardo's famous multiple-imposition of a human body—shown with arms and legs stretched rigidly to describe a square and also angled to fill a circle—comes directly from the work of Vitruvius. The masters of antiquity had learned not only the correct proportions of torso, limbs, and parts, but the magic of portraying the body as something flexible—a form that moves, through the shifting of weight; altered through tension and relaxation; dependent on a balance of axes. Donatello, Brunelleschi's friend and companion on his search through Rome's artifacts, revived this approach in his own works with breathtaking success, especially in his startling and exquisite nude sculpture of David.

As early as the first century B.C.E., Lucretius outlined concepts similar to those described in Alberti's eye-opening fifteenth-century method book on perspective. With the fall of the ancient world, however, much of this approach had been discarded. And when the illusion of depth crept back into the picture in the later Middle Ages, it was only through imprecise contrivances like "tonal atmosphere," created by contrasts of color, shade, and light. Paintings like Giotto's *Herod's Feast* and Ambrogio Lorenzetti's *The Presentation in the Temple* in the fourteenth century demonstrated the possibilities latent in the skillful tampering of spatial relations; but their creators had little more to go on than raw talent and intuition.

By 1400, theorist Cennino Cennini had begun reaching for a more methodical approach, based on what Giotto had accomplished. In the same year, the manuscript of Ptolemy's 1,300-year-old *Geographia* became available in Florence, offering lessons in how to depict a curved map on a flat surface. Ptolemy's maps could be wildly inaccurate, but the achievement was impressive nonetheless. It took Brunelleschi and his followers, however, to bring this art to a new level of mathematical certainty: men like Masaccio, whose fresco *The Trinity* conveyed depth so realistically that the painting appeared—according to biographer Giorgio Vasari—"to have holes in it"; and Alberti, who spread word of the new mathematically based perspective system through his 1435 treatise *On Painting.* Here at last was a reliable road to man's conquest of space.

Once again, as Petrarch warned about the work of Giotto, great minds were "greatly taken" with the results. Vasari recorded an extreme case: It seems that the painter Paolo Uccello spent so many of his nights poring over perspective theories that his wife pleaded with him to come to bed. His only response was, "What a delightful thing is this perspective!" (In fairness, however, it must be stated that no known portrait of Mrs. Uccello survives.)

Perspective painting quickly moved beyond mere technique to become something deeper: a mode of wrestling with reality, of learning to parse nature's ways and then to restate them into a language of points and planes. Art begat science.

And science in turn helped bring art to new heights. "Those [artists] who are enamored of practice without science," Leonardo explained, "are like sailors who board a ship without rudder and compass, never having any certainty as to whither they go." And if any Renaissance figure appeared to have an unfailing compass, it was Leonardo. The man came to personify the new spirit of inquiry. He wanted to know not only the workings of the eye, but why birds can fly, and how the earth generates mountains and rivers. He pondered the sun: Why does the fiery ball appear larger when rising or setting than when it is at its full height in the sky? He declared that the spheres moving through the heavens do not make a sound, and addressed the question of whether it was the blacksmith's hammer or anvil that created the musical tones that had intrigued Pythagoras.

He began dissecting corpses long before physicians considered it worthwhile. Indeed, the practice was viewed as unwholesome, at best. Vasari recounted several cautionary tales of the time: of the young Aretine painter Bartolommeo Torri, who kept the limbs of dead men under his bed until a stench permeated the whole house; and of Silvio Cosini, who stole the corpse of a hanged man from its grave in order to dissect it, then succumbed to the urge to make a coat of its skin, "thinking it had magical power."

But Leonardo was unlikely to get caught up in such superstitious behavior; scientific inquiry had shaped him into the most practical man on earth. While still in the service of Verrocchio he developed a loathing for angelic figures, because he concluded that the back and shoulder muscles of the angels as portrayed couldn't possibly operate both arms and wings at the same time. He detested fraud wherever he found it: How many others of his generation clamored to have all the astrologers castrated? Even Pope Innocent VIII fell under their spell; the pontiff implored the ruler of Milan, Lodovico Sforza, to lend him the celebrated astrologer Ambrogio da Rosate so he could have his personal horoscope drawn up. There were, of course, a few other skeptics. The philosopher Pico della Mirandola, for example, kept a weather diary in the 1480s and found that astrological predictions were correct only 7 percent of the time. (Yet, one can't help wondering how many contemporary meteorologists might happily flaunt that kind of record.)

Today, after all these centuries, the fruits of Leonardo's labors still evoke an air of modernity: scissors that can be opened and closed with one hand; an adjustable monkey wrench; three-speed transmission gears; the machine gun; the parachute; inflated skis for walking on water. (More mundane matters could also engage his problem-solving faculties. Once, when he stumbled upon a house of ill repute, Leonardo was so struck by the impracticality of its design that he quickly drew up new building plans with an intricate system of corridors, to allow customers to slip in and out unnoticed.)

And some of Leonardo's most innovative devices were musical instruments. There was a fantastic silver fiddle in the shape of a horse's skull; a keyboard that produced sounds like a string orchestra; a flute in which the tones would glide from one to another, like those in a latter-day electronic theremin. He was, reported contemporaries, one of the greatest musicians of his age, especially when performing on the Renaissance fiddle known as the *lira da braccio* (an instrument Galileo's father, Vincenzo Galilei, later called the *lira moderna*).

He was an improviser—the best of his day, both as a lira player and as a creator of spontaneous rhymes—and the lira da braccio was the instrument of choice for improvisers. It was favored by many courtly Italian poet-musicians, who used it to accompany their extemporaneous poetry and narratives; these included the influential philosopher Marsilio

Ficino as well as painters like Raphael and Leonardo. The instrument was perfect for chordal playing—the sounding of several tones simultaneously in an agreeable blend of thirds and fifths—and extant music for the lira emphasizes this trait. There was an extramusical reason behind its popularity as well: The lira was assumed to have an ancient lineage, and was often depicted in the hands of Orpheus, Apollo, Sappho, Homer, or King David. Leonardo must have been keenly aware of the dramatic potential of the instrument. It was shaped something like a violin, but among its seven strings there were two used for unchanging drones, a feature associated today more with Eastern instruments or bagpipes. It was, in addition, held in a manner today's violinists would consider unbecoming, with the fingerboard pointing downward.

Leonardo's strange silver instrument in the shape of a horse's skull was a lira da braccio. When he played it for Lorenzo de' Medici, the powerful ruler was so amazed at the sight and sound of the instrument he sent Leonardo, along with his friend the singer Atalante Migliorotti, to Milan to present it as a gift to Duke Lodovico Sforza. The bizarre shape of Leonardo's lira undoubtedly accounted for part of its appeal, but it was probably not the only impressive thing about the instrument, which was reported to have an unusually rich tone.

Many instruments of the time—and instrumentalists too, it seems—were far less bland than those of today. A lira da braccio by Giovanni d'Andrea of Verona, dated 1511 and now residing in the Kunsthistorisches Museum in Vienna, has a belly in the shape of a male torso, with the front of its peg box depicting a hideous male face; the reverse side portrays a female figure. What's more, Lorenzo was said to be unusually discerning in musical matters. Once, when the accomplished organ builder Antonio Squarcialupi was disparaged in his presence, Lorenzo replied, "If you knew what it means to be supreme in any field, you would be more lenient in your judgment of him." He must have recognized the sound of Leonardo's silver lira to be especially inspiring.

In fact, each of Leonardo's musical inventions seemed to break new ground in extending an instrument's expressive possibilities. The *viola organista* was his attempt to overcome the limitations of the harpsichord, which, because the strings were plucked, could not vary in volume even if a player changed the amount of pressure used on the keys. (The clavichord allowed such a change in volume by having a brass blade strike its strings in direct proportion to the force of the player—as did its cousin the *dulce melos,* or keyed dulcimer— but each produced a meager sound.)

Leonardo's solution was to design an instrument with constantly rotating friction wheels that rubbed against the strings. Increasing and decreasing the pressure of these wheels on the strings could vary the instrument's volume at a finger's touch. The viola organista was in some ways a descendant of the organistrum of the tenth, eleventh, and twelfth centuries (attributed to Oddo of Cluny)—a two-man instrument made with a wheel and crank—and of the hurdy-gurdy, a mechanical fiddle popular in the later Middle Ages that was vilified by composer Michael Praetorius in the seventeenth century as the lyre of peasants and itinerant wenches.

The viola organista, and descendants of it, surfaced in various forms for quite a while. In 1581, Vincenzo Galilei mentioned a similar keyboard instrument with bowed strings, which sounded like an "ensemble of viols." In 1618 Praetorius devoted a whole chapter in his *Treatise on Music* to similar contraptions. Most striking of all, an official inventory of the Medici collection listed just such a keyboard with the ability to vary the intensity of its sound; it had five wheels. The keeper of that collection (and the signer of its official inventory) was Bartolomeo Cristofori, the man credited today with the invention of the piano, a keyboard instrument hailed as revolutionary for its responsiveness to a player's varying touch.

Leonardo's approaches to creating better musical instruments were informed by his studies of living organisms. He often based his improvements, for example, on what he knew of human anatomy: the workings of the larynx, the movements of hand and finger tendons. In his view, man, music, nature, and art were all links in one great chain of being. Indeed, he found the connections between vision and hearing particularly evident. Leonardo found parallels between the tendency of people to perceive landscapes on a wall spotted with stains, for example, and their inclination to hear names or words in the peals of a clanging bell. He found analogies between the behavior of distant light and that of fading sounds. And he saw inextricable bonds between art and the natural world.

Strike a table with a hammer, and small heaps of dust collect into mounds on its surface. From such vibrations, he concluded, the particles of the earth give birth to hills, just as the "waves of sand carried by the wind" create mountains in Libya. Music and nature were perpetually joined in a great dancing resonance. (Three hundred years later, Ernst Florens

The Harmony of Heaven and Earth

Friedrich Chladni would describe how the hum created by the movement of a bow across a flexible plate causes the grains of sand sitting on top to form geometric patterns, called "tone figures.")

In the same way, he believed, the earth is profoundly linked to man. Its soil is a kind of flesh, he determined; "the rocks which form the mountains are its bones . . . and the waters its blood. . . . The ebb and flow of the ocean is its breathing. . . . The swelling of the spirit of growth is in the fires which burst forth in various parts of the world in hot springs, in sulfur mines and volcanoes. . . ." The famous portrait of Mona Lisa (*La Gioconda*) makes the relationship explicit: The winding rivers of the painting's background whisper their presence in the falling strands of Mona Lisa's hair, which gently undulate with the rhythm of a murmuring stream. Leonardo himself pointed to the way her attire continues the analogy, in "the little rivulets of drapery falling from her gathered neckline."

A vital connection between music and painting was equally clear. Since painting serves the eye, wrote Leonardo, "there arises from it a harmony of proportions"—just like those in music, where different voices joining together create such pleasurable sensations "that the listeners remain struck with admiration as if half alive." As a painter, Leonardo claimed, he determined the distances between objects by the rules a musician uses to determine the distances between tones.

And yet, the rules of proportion in Leonardo's paintings were no longer simply a matter of surrendering to heavenly ideals, or even of achieving a precise imitation of reality. There was, in them, a new kind of creative synthesis at work.

Temperament

As a full participant with nature in God's grand scheme, man—the measure of all things—demanded a special kind of harmony, one that would, said Leonardo, render him "struck with admiration." It was the kind of reaction Leonardo could generate as a masterful musician. Now he brought that experience to bear in his paintings. An example can be found in his brilliant rendering of the Last Supper. It sits on the north wall of the dining room of the convent of Santa Maria delle Grazie in Milan.

The scene of Jesus and his disciples at their final meal is intended to look as if it were taking place in an extension of the dining room itself. However, the logic of the scene is subverted at every turn. Leonardo uses the technique of perspective to draw the viewer's vision not straight across the hall but upward, toward the head of Christ, about fifteen feet above the ground, as if a spectator were being levitated into the Savior's presence. The painting's table is drawn in an unrealistically long and narrow fashion, and it is unable to accommodate chairs for all of the disciples, who are crammed together into a jumble of torsos and limbs. And yet there is a poetic harmony to the clotted images that can be felt in the surging wave traced by the disciples' faces as they crest and fall rhythmically across the painting's horizon, and in the musical proportions used for the diminishing tapestries that recede along the image's walls.

The dazzling power of *The Last Supper* results not from arbitrary choice, but from careful calculation—toward an end. Leonardo scrupulously calibrated the angles, lines, and light that flowed from his brushes, playing with proportional relationships in order to create a special effect. Many of his contemporaries were doing the same—and not only the painters. During the first half of the fifteenth century cho-reographing dancers into patterns so that they would evoke certain qualities (such as "airy presence," or supple rhythm, described as "slowness compensated by quickness") became a new rage in Italy. (The earliest known treatise on this sub-ject, by Domenico da Piacenza, was written in the 1440s.) And the same process was becoming paramount for key-board musicians.

The mathematics of ideal beauty inherited from Py-thagoras were no longer viable. Thirds played in the Pythag-orean tuning—that is, the tuning created through a series of perfect fifths—were grating and often unusable (and for that reason long considered dissonances to be avoided). But tuning a keyboard to produce only pure thirds was equally untenable—it created a system at war with itself, unable to render the all-important musical sounds of perfect octaves and fifths.

So, like the painters, musicians searched for an accommo-dation between the ideal and the practical, for a way to *refor-mulate the proportions* between musical tones so they would produce desirable effects as they coalesced on the canvas of time. They wanted a new harmony of parts. They needed a recipe for *musical perspective*.

The answer was temperament.

8

A Keyboard Perspective

> If the true concord of well-tuned sounds,
> By unions married, do offend thine ear,
> They do but sweetly chide thee, who confounds
> In singleness the parts that thou shouldst bear.
>
> —William Shakespeare, Sonnet 8

Temperament. It derives from the Latin *temperare,* "to tamper with," and the French *tempérer,* "to mix ingredients proportionately," to produce a favorable blending of contraries. It also comes from Old English *temprian,* "to regulate": God turns the spheres and tempers all on high. To temper can mean to adjust to the needs of a situation, to ease difficulty by finding a middle course or forging a compromise.

To temper is to make morally suitable, as in *temperance,* and to instill peace, as in *temperamentum:* the due measure that leads to balance. A healthy temperament, it was once believed, results from the equilibrium of various physical humors. Tempering is an act that persuades and pacifies.

"Now will I do to that old Andronicus, and temper him with all the art I have," wrote Shakespeare. Men temper themselves through restraint to avoid the explosive outbursts of *distemper.*

Other related words suggest broader connections. There is *tempus:* to do things at the right time, in the right season. And there is *templum:* a space cut off and consecrated to the gods—the origin of *temple.* Each term connotes a world partitioned into dissimilar fragments, then made whole through a process of judicious blending.

Musical temperament was a response to the frustrating discovery that nature's proportions, in spite of man's best efforts to force them into a regimented, reliable scheme, follow their own inexorable paths. In application, it is similar to the Japanese art of *bonsai.*

The practice of cultivating miniature trees acquired its name from two Chinese words, denoting "scenery" and "container." Its artistry lies in vigilantly controlling the trunk, branches, and leaves of a tree as it grows—balancing nature's asymmetry with a sculptor's sense of form. The practitioner of bonsai perceives that a solitary branch left free to follow its own contour will shine with an individual grace and beauty. But as a single element joining with others to produce a perfectly contained figure, it must be pruned or in other ways forced to assume a particular shape. Music's incompatible proportions created an unclipped bonsai. Temperament would provide the clippers.

Tempering blends music's essential building blocks by pruning or reshaping them. It was a necessary compromise forged in the face of defeat. Even tunings that managed to yield selected pure thirds, fifths, and octaves all at the same time—like the one concocted by Spanish theorist Bartolomeo Ramos de Pareja in 1482—failed to relieve the problem faced by musicians who were encountering wolves at every turn. Indeed, each new attempt at reaching a tuning that would be practical and yet preserve the revered concordances did little more than provoke yet another ideological brawl.

Ramos was a case in point: a troublemaker who railed against music's greatest authorities, Boethius and Guido of Arezzo. He objected to the way music was notated and to the way it was vocalized. He complained about the ill-sounding thirds produced by the standard Pythagorean tuning, which was based on perfect fifths. He unleashed a flood of arguments that continued to swirl between his adversaries and disciples well into the sixteenth century.

Ramos's feistiness leaps off the page. Of his critics, he wrote, "I wish to destroy the head, so that the whole body of errors becomes a corpse and cannot live any longer." In large part, the argument that ensued between Ramos and his antagonists was a theological one. Under his assault, the very ground on which church music had been built threatened to collapse. Addressing the belief that musical rhythm organized in groups of three was the most "perfect," for example—owing to its intimation of the Holy Trinity—Ramos was typically scornful. "It is a defect to want to prove something in mathematical disciplines through analogy," he sneered.

His opponents included a priest named Nicolaus Burtius, who authored a pamphlet "against a Spanish prevaricator of the truth." If the old ways were good enough for Gregory, Ambrose, and Augustine, asked Burtius, "why don't you blush to pervert this order . . . ? Are you perhaps more saintly than these pillars of the Church or more cultivated or more experienced?" It's easy to guess Ramos's answer. "I don't fear a fight," he once declared. Inevitably, however, he was forced to leave Bologna, never to publish again.

Among his innovations, Ramos advocated a new way of dividing the string length of the instrument still favored by theorists for their acoustical experiments—Pythagoras's single-string monochord. He did this, he explained, to relieve the plight of singers for whom the Pythagorean way was just too complicated and cumbersome. His new system created an interesting result. Many of the fifths it produced between the tones of his musical scale retained the lovely, perfect consonance they enjoyed in Pythagoras's tuning. Yet many of the thirds—unusable in Pythagoras's tuning—now sounded their most harmonious as well. The name given to a system that yields both pure fifths and pure thirds in the same musical scale is *just intonation*. The idea behind it is at least as old as the second century, where it appeared in the writings of the astronomer and philosopher Claudius Ptolemy.

Still, just intonation offered little solace to troubled keyboard players. A little musical geometry shows why.

Like all instrumental tunings, just intonation begins with an inviolable rule: The octave must be pure. *Do* reaches to *do* like an image meeting its reflection; together they define the edges of the musical world. And not merely the edges: Pietro Aron, one of the sixteenth century's most important musicians, saw the octave as "so pure, so full, so perfect before all intervals, that not only all voices, but also all other consonances flow together into this one as their leader, they subject themselves to it as to their prince, they revere and receive it as moderator of each concord and as queen. . . . It releases all possible consonances like a fertile mother. . . ."

Temperament

The octave, as we've seen, is created when two strings are in the ratio 2:1.

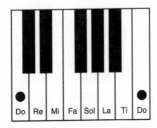

With these boundaries in place, we can begin to fill in the other missing pitches. To provide our keyboard with *just intonation,* a pure fifth above the *do* is produced by a string whose length forms the proportion 3:2 with the string for *do.*

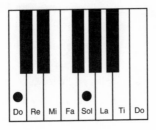

And a "pure" major third is provided above *do* through the proportion 5:4.

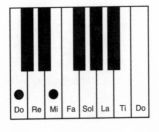

A Keyboard Perspective

The interval of a fourth above *do* may be established through a string length with which it forms the ratio 4:3.

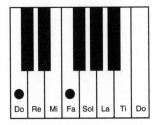

This leaves three scale tones to be filled in. From *do* to *ti* is a seventh (starting on *do*, *ti* is the seventh member of the scale). However, this tone also forms a major third above *sol*, and that makes it easy to calculate. We can use a string whose length in relation to *sol* forms the proportion 5:4. Likewise, *la* can be found by calculating a major third above *fa*.

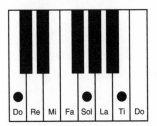

The one remaining scale tone is *re*. We can find it by calculating a fourth below *sol*.

The justly tuned scale is now complete. But it is rife with problems. Some of the musical tones have been calculated using the proportion of a perfect fifth; others have been calculated using the proportion of a major third. These differing formulations create intervals of different sizes, so that the individual musical steps on this keyboard will not be uniform. When all of the proportions are calculated, it turns out that the distance between *do* and *re,* for example, is not the same as that between *re* and *mi.* This same inconsistency pops up when measuring the distance between *fa* and *sol* against the span between *sol* and *la.*

And the musical consequences can be severe. Certain harmonies sound exquisitely pure on a justly tuned keyboard—the chords that result from adding a major third and a perfect fifth above *do,* or *fa,* or *sol,* for example.

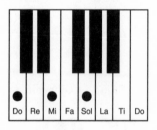

However, building a similar chord on *re* spells disaster. We have chosen our *la* to sound a beautiful major third above *fa,* and because of that the proportion formed between *re* and *la* will not create a perfect fifth—the distance between these two tones will be shorter than the "pure" fifth created through the proportion 3:2. So striking the scale members *re, fa,* and *la* together—despite our anticipation of an agreeable outcome—will now create a hideous, unmusical racket.

Yet, readjusting these intervals—by changing the pitch of *re,* for example, altering its distance from *la* so that the two tones form a proper fifth—would automatically corrupt the harmony we may wish to build on *sol.* The conflict is irresolvable.

A Keyboard Perspective

Some musicians—including Leonardo da Vinci's friend the composer, teacher, and priest Franchinus Gaffurius—vociferously objected to Ramos's approach and continued to defend the standard Pythagorean tuning. However, while each side in the debate was busily staking its claim for musical correctness, yet another profound development had already unfolded. Both Ramos and Gaffurius make mention of it in their writings. Gaffurius reported in his *Practica musica* (completed in 1483) that organists of his time were, through an adjustment to the lengths of their organ pipes, diminishing the proportions used to create their fifths, "by a very small and hidden and somewhat uncertain quantity." The practice was called *temperament* (or *participata*).

On its face, the description seems nebulous—and of little import. But Gaffurius's *"participata,"* like Archimedes' *"Eureka!"* heralds a finding of breathtaking significance. The fact is, the organists in the story, unlike Ramos or Gaffurius, were not seeking a "perfect" tuning at all. Instead, they had adopted a different goal altogether: one of utility. In their crusade to overcome the keyboardists' dilemma, they had redrawn the battle lines: For music's sake, the principle of maintaining purity had given way to a strategy of acceptable loss. To create a more serviceable instrument, they had decided to sacrifice the sanctity of the fifths.

For some, this change must have been as alarming as the thought of hacking out the central beam of a house—an action that might cause the entire structure to collapse on everyone inside. However, there was an elegant reasoning behind the practice.

As we have already seen, in an instrument tuned in the traditional way, through a series of perfect fifths, the harmony of the third will be unpalatable, like a splash of vinegar in the ears. We can produce this unsatisfactory third by imitating the procedure Pythagoras followed when building a series of fifths on his monochord. After fixing our *do,* we install the string for the tone a fifth above—*sol.* From *sol,* we repeat the process, and find the string for the *re* that lies a perfect fifth above it, and so on. Thus we find our pitches for the tones *do, sol, re, la,* and *mi* (and then locate their octave counterparts across the keyboard).

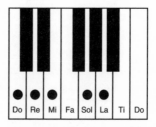

When the process is finished, we have created a situation in which the major third from *do* to *mi* is not the pure third preferred by the ears. This third is wider than a *just* third (that is, than the pure third produced by the ratio 5:4) by a tiny amount—a gap called the *didymic* or *syntonic comma.* But suppose we found a way to shorten automatically the span of this Pythagorean third—to eliminate the comma—so that it sounds just right? One way to accomplish this would be by removing a little piece from each of the four building blocks we used to find *mi*—that is, by shortening the length of each perfect fifth by one quarter of the amount of the comma. A stack of these four shortened fifths would now yield a *mi* that would create just the right size third. And though the fifth can endure only so much tampering before it becomes a howling "wolf," its reduction by only a small fraction of that comma is tolerable to most listeners. This way of adjusting the old tuning based on perfect fifths created a new tuning, known as *mean-tone temperament.*

Mean-tone temperament had definite advantages over the old approach, though it also carried its own set of problems. The wolf fifth, for instance—that odd, ugly interval that must be used somewhere to round out the circle of all twelve tones—still lurks within this system. However, mean-tone offered a stability lacking in Ramos's just intonation system: It is more uniform. The intervals *do–re* and *re–mi*, for example, are now of the same size. Unfortunately, half-steps—the shortest distances found on the instrument, such as those between *do* and the black note immediately to its right, *do-sharp;* or between *re* and the black note immediately to its right, *mi-flat*—are still of differing sizes.

Such irregularities in the distances between tones had severely limited the scope of just intonation's usefulness, and *mean-tone* temperament had clearly extended an instrument's range of possibility; nevertheless, calamitous effects could still occur. Play a major *triad* (a three-note chord consisting of a tone along with the major third and the fifth above it) beginning on *sol.* In the one-quarter-comma mean-tone tuning described above, the result is glorious.

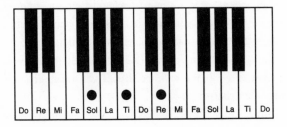

But shift that entire combination of tones up one half-step—that is, begin this same three-toned structure on the black note immediately to the right of *sol, sol-sharp*—and the result will sound like a set of fine china dinnerware crashing to the floor.

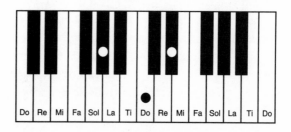

This is because *sol-sharp* may be tuned to be either a pure major third in relation to *mi* or a fourth in relation to *mi-flat* (the note immediately to the left of *mi*)—but not both. Only one of these combinations will work; in the end, some harmonies simply have to be sacrificed. Some music did not require such disparate harmonies in the same piece, and could of course be performed in mean-tone temperament with eloquent results. But when a composition began in one tonal region and then shifted to another, the music could still howl and bray like a barnyard tempest.

One solution to this problem was to offer extra keys, giving the performer a choice of playing either *la-flat* or *sol-sharp*. Ramos made mention of this approach as well, and a 1480 contract for a cathedral organ at Lucca specified the installation of such a device. The idea would gain new adherents over time, as we will see. But it was cumbersome, and ultimately unsatisfactory.

Diminishing the fifths by exactly one-quarter of the

A Keyboard Perspective

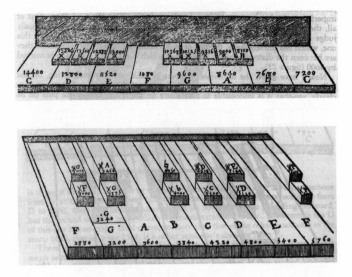

Keyboards with seventeen keys to the octave and nineteen keys to the octave, from Marin Mersenne's *Harmonie universelle* (1636–37)

comma during the tuning process was actually only one option out of many pursued by musicians. The fifteenth and sixteenth centuries sprouted literally hundreds of varieties of mean-tone temperament. In fact, a single composer might invent dozens of individual tunings—some customized to fit particular pieces, others offered as musical "flavorings" to be tried willy-nilly. (The term *mean-tone* was used, in each case, to signify the uniform size of whole steps, like the distances from *do* to *re* and from *re* to *mi*, which were found by splitting the span between *do* and *mi* in half—in other words, by finding its mean.) Some musicians invented tuning formulas that compromised the fifths exclusively; others tweaked both the fifths and the thirds. Some temperaments were consistent in their adjustments, but many were asymmetric, altering, for example, certain selected fifths more than others.

Temperaments soon became the musical equivalent of poet Robert Frost's notion of a sentence. "A sentence," Frost wrote to John Bartlett, "is a sound in itself on which other sounds called words may be strung." Temperaments were sentences—or distinctive sound-worlds—through which notes strung as melodies and harmonies became suffused with particular shades and shapes. Their in-tuneness and out-of-tuneness, the special atmospheres their intervals conveyed, the forces they exerted on the musical direction within a piece—all combined to produce a kind of *perspective* in sound: a filter through which an artist's tonal point of view was projected.

In the sixteenth century, as a cartography rage swept over Europe, mean-tone temperaments proliferated like maps of musical neighborhoods. In place of the compass and plane used by mapmakers to detail the roads and canals of towns and cities, musicians used their tuning tools to imprint on their instruments the shapes of key musical landmarks and the narrow paths that wound between them.

Myriad opinions arose about how that musical map should be rendered. Such disagreements were predictable, of course, in this new cultural era, a time vitally shaped by the ascent of the individual.

9

Euclid's Gift

The world's great age begins anew,
    The Golden years return,
The earth doth like a snake renew
    Her winter weeds outworn:
Heaven smiles, and faiths and empires gleam
Like wrecks of a dissolving dream.

        —Percy Bysshe Shelley, "From Hellas"

Life's hungry man" is the way Thomas Wolfe once described an artist: "the glutton of eternity, beauty's miser, glory's slave." His words could well have described the spirit of an entire age. The Renaissance was a wellspring of artistic vision—voracious in its appetite for beauty, enchanted by the lure of timeless truth, and greedy in its pursuit of eminence.

It was an era shaped by men like Florentine ruler Lorenzo de' Medici, known as Lorenzo the Magnificent. At the age of nineteen, while testing his skills in the arts of war by entering a tournament and winning—"not by favor," he would later brag, but by "valor"—Lorenzo wore armor emblazoned with the French motto "Le temps revient": The [Golden] Age Returns. He spent the rest of his life making good that promise.

Reclaiming the glory of the past, when cities were regal and men were sage, became a consuming passion for the legion of artists, musicians, and scholars in Lorenzo's employ. He commissioned translations of the classics written by Horace, Homer, Virgil, Pliny the Elder, and Dante; restored the University of Pisa; even sustained the Platonic Academy at Florence begun by his grandfather Cosimo, where the philosopher, doctor, and musician Marsilio Ficino held court. Ficino became so enamored of the ancient masters he was translating that he began the habit of greeting his students as "beloved in Plato" rather than "beloved in Christ."

A new movable-type printing press developed by Johannes Gutenberg eased the dissemination of each new find. This mechanical marvel was hailed by Erasmus as "the greatest of all inventions." It incited a less than enthusiastic response in other quarters; professional copyists opposed it, for obvious reasons, along with aristocrats who feared that their libraries would decrease in value. Some clergy also dreaded the spread of subversive thought they correctly predicted in its wake. But theirs was a minority opinion. "What a century! What literature! How good it is to be alive!" wrote Ulrich von Hüteen in 1518 in a letter to famed humanist Willibald Pirckheimer.

Nearly every facet of society was touched by these pursuits. Five years before von Hüteen's famous letter, Machiavelli—in exile and beginning work on his masterpiece of political ruthlessness, *The Prince*—found nightly consolation in the emerging voices of the past. "I go into the library," he wrote, "and as I cross the threshold I cast off my everyday clothing, covered with filth and mud, and put on the costume of the royal court. . . . Thus honorably clad, I enter the classical court of the Ancients. They welcome me warmly, and I feast on the nourishment for which I was born. . . ."

Even the church succumbed to the craze. Pope Nicholas V gathered a collection of more than a thousand volumes in Greek and Latin—the core of the future Vatican Library—and initiated the rebuilding of Rome. But on his deathbed in 1455, Nicholas disclosed a very practical reason behind it all: "To create solid and stable convictions in the minds of the uncultured masses, there must be something that appeals to the eye," he explained. "A popular faith, sustained only on doctrines, will never be anything but feeble and vacillating." Under Nicholas the old calls for austerity were now a distant echo. The road to salvation would be paved with feasts for the eyes and ears, not merely injunctions for the soul. If the artists Botticelli and Leonardo could turn to Lorenzo for financial support, so Raphael and Michelangelo would find it at the door of the Holy See.

The Jubilee Year of 1450 provided an example of just how profitable church spectacles could be. A celebration planned around the inauguration of the pope on Christmas Day, 1449, drew tens of thousands of pilgrims to Rome. Despite a plague that left the roads lined with corpses and a disastrous stampede caused by a bucking mule—at least two hundred people were trampled to death or drowned in the Tiber—offerings by visitors allowed the pope to deposit 100,000 gold florins in the Medici bank. (The commotion was par for the course. In the *Inferno,* Dante depicted the very first jubilee, held in 1300, as a traffic jam in Hell.)

In the contest for power, however, the secular authorities were now clearly in the ascendance. Lorenzo, flexing his political muscles, even mused over the religious schism that had not long before convulsed the church, and noted wryly that there were advantages in having three or even four popes at a time. Ironically, in 1513, long after Lorenzo's death, his son Giovanni would become Pope Leo X.

The treasures of antiquity held a different allure for philosopher Marsilio Ficino and his compatriots at the Platonic Academy than they had for Pope Nicholas V. The latter found them a useful tool for promoting church doctrine. Ficino's role was more that of a spiritual archaeologist, burrowing for something deeper—a lost connection to the divine mysteries. One day the prize he was seeking suddenly arrived at his doorstep in the form of a manuscript. Obtained by Cosimo de' Medici from a traveling monk, its contents were attributed to an enigmatic figure known as Hermes Trismegistus. Ficino could hardly believe his luck. Here, he thought, was the written work of Trismegistus of Egypt, the nephew of Mercury and seer of dark arts, the ancient purveyor of wisdom who roamed the sands with Moses, Atlas, and Prometheus. The words were like the flickers of an ancient candle. They set his soul on fire.

In truth, the manuscript was more likely a more recent work, written by a scholar familiar with both Plato and the Bible. Nevertheless, Ficino was convinced that he held in his hands a message from the very first theologian, the founder of a lineage that led successively through Orpheus, Aglaophemus, Pythagoras, Philolaus, and, finally, to Plato himself. He dedicated his life to translating it.

As Ficino's rich find further stoked the philosophical fires, Christian scholars, convinced that Jewish sources would provide further support for their evolving theology, began to tap those roots as well. Actually, the two religions had already borrowed freely from one another: Thomas Aquinas smoothly adopted aspects of Maimonides' *Guide for the Perplexed,* for example, just as the Jewish philosophers Judah Romano and David, the son of Messer Leon, freely foraged Aquinas's *Summa Theologica.* Nevertheless, when a member of Ficino's circle, philosopher Pico della Mirandola, decided to delve deeply into the Jewish mystical tradition known as kabbalah, he was treading on dangerous ground. The conjoining of so many disparate influences was bound to make for a combustible mix, and Pico's production of nine hundred stunningly provocative theses—including the assertion that God spoke through pagans as well as through prophets— was more than Rome could endure. Theology was in danger of fracturing into a chaos of individual interpretation. Pico's condemnation was swift. And a countercurrent was set in motion. In 1509, Johannes Pfefferkorn, a rabbi turned Dominican monk, warned of the hazards inherent in such pursuits and proposed in his tract *Mirror of the Jews* that all works written in Hebrew be destroyed. (It didn't happen until 1553, when copies of the Talmud in Italy were finally ordered confiscated and burned.)

Within this ferment of clashing convictions, the hunt was continuing for a Holy Grail of music. As Ficino translated the third-century philosopher Plotinus, he became intrigued by a description of how one string in a musical instrument often "trembles at the vibration of another, as if the second string felt the first" (a fact that also fascinated Leonardo da Vinci). This kind of motion is conveyed from one lyre to another, reasoned Plotinus, as a result of a mutually felt harmony, in the same way the universe is home to but a single harmony arising from opposites. Ficino pondered the idea and began applying the principle to his practice as a healer. Body and soul, he concluded, join in harmony through a certain musical proportion—dictated by the vibrations of Apollo's lyre. The final section of his medical treatise *De vita* is entitled "On Obtaining Life from the Heavens."

Pico della Mirandola's mentor and companion, Rabbi Yohanan Alemanno, also found ample support in the annals of Jewish mysticism for the view that music contains a spiritual force. Rabbi Isaac ben Jacob ha-Kohen, a thirteenth-century kabbalist from Castile, for example, likened musicians who properly direct their fingers over the holes and strings of their instruments to the high priest who awakens the Holy Spirit through prayer. In Pico's own time, Spanish rabbi Meir ibn Gabbai explained in his treatise *Avodat ha-Qodesh* that in the proper performance of music, a magical resonance occurs between earth and heaven: "Because just as I am arousing here below, so the arousal will also be on high. . . ." This secret, Meir revealed, is symbolized in a famous ancient icon: not the lyre of Apollo, but "the harp of David."

These ideas, however lofty sounding, actually affected musical practice: Bartolomeo Ramos de Pareja's tuning innovations grew out of a worldview very close to Ficino's. Ramos, likely inspired by Arabic texts in his native Spain, was convinced that certain musical scales had the power to move the bodily humors—influencing sluggishness, or balancing anger and pride, or moderating sadness and joy. "Music works miracles," he asserted, citing the legendary Greek musicians who were able to "move wild beasts through the sweetness of their song, to capture the hearts of men, to revive the dead, to bend to mercy the spirits of the under-world, to draw trees from the mountains." For Ramos, the rules defining the relations between musical tones were, in effect, a prescription for soundness of body and mind.

Those rules, however, like so much that had once rested securely on a central authority, were now a matter of open debate. And the dialogue was beginning to heat up. While theorists sparred over the merits of Pythagorean, just, and mean-tone systems, yet another front surfaced in the tuning wars, this one led by a daring composer named Adrian Willaert. His opening salvo was a vocal piece in four parts, written in 1519.

Willaert's *Quid non ebrietas* shattered convention. The piece opens in an ordinary fashion, using harmonies built from the tones of the *do* scale. In the beginning, *do* serves as the work's central tone—the hub around which all the musi-cal lines will orbit. The musical scale that begins and ends on *do* thus serves as the music's framework. But Willaert's voices never settle down for long. Within moments, the tenor part, twisting and turning in unexpected directions, snakes its way toward another tonal center, with a different constellation of scale tones; then it moves on to yet another. Every time the music seems to fix itself around one particu-lar point, it swerves abruptly, winding this way and that, sleekly traveling through unexpected pathways, alighting for a brief moment on every one of the twelve distinct tones

Pythagoras found in his chain of perfect fifths. Finally, it concludes its journey with an octave leap.

This is music fraught with dangers—almost impossible to perform. Even the simple concluding octave could not easily be executed. Willaert had slyly placed an enormous obstacle in its way: All through the piece, as a performer steered his part through different tonal centers, he would unavoidably run headlong into musical commas at every turn—the irreconcilable gaps that result from the fact that fifths, octaves, and thirds are all based on different standards of measure. Each gap would set the singer slightly off course. The music would inevitably drift out of tune, leading to bad-sounding intervals, just as it would on a keyboard with fixed strings.

Striving to make the first and last tones of *Quid non ebrietas* agree was like trying to fill a gallon tank exactly to the brim by alternately emptying quart jars and liter containers into it. The differing proportions of these receptacles will always prevent them from arriving at the same level. In the end, the tank will either overflow or be partially empty. When sung in Pythagorean tuning, Willaert's melody concludes with a disastrously ugly leap, an interval slightly *larger* than a pure octave; it overflows. Using just intonation, on the other hand—because of *that* tuning's particular irregularities—produces in the Willaert piece a final jump slightly *short* of a pure octave; the melody leaves its container unsatisfactorily empty. The composer purposely designed this music so that it would fail with either system. It would succeed flawlessly, however, with a radical tuning called equal temperament.

The idea would have been considered preposterous only a few decades earlier. In equal temperament the octave is divided into twelve completely uniform parts. Medieval and early Renaissance theorists denied that such a thing was even possible. The great authority in these matters, Boethius, had declared the notion absurd: After all, a whole step—say, the distance from *do* to *re*—is produced by two strings in the ratio 9:8. This couldn't possibly be evenly divided, because the attempt would yield an irrational number—a number that never ends. Thus, there is no clear middle point at which that intervening black note, *do-sharp*, can be placed.

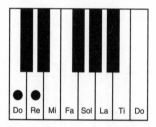

Obviously, concluded Boethius, since you can't find a proportion that slices *do* to *re* exactly in half, the musical distance from *do* to the black note immediately to its right, *do-sharp*, cannot be the same as the distance from *do-sharp* to *re*. One of those half-steps (the shortest distance between any two notes on the keyboard) must be formed by the ratio 18:17, and the other by the ratio 17:16. Added together, they will then produce the proper ratio for the whole step from *do* to *re*: 9:8. No other solution is possible.

Or so it seemed. That argument was vanquished only with the publication in 1482 of a translation of Euclid's *Elements*. With Euclid's help, a *geometric* solution to the quandary was possible—a way of solving this untidy mathematical problem not through heady calculation, but with semicircles and perpendiculars. Applied to a monochord, Euclid's method could find the mean proportion between any two lengths of string: octaves, thirds, whole tones.

Nevertheless, dividing the octave into twelve equal parts remained a bit of a problem; using Euclid's approach, one could split this span into two, four, or even sixteen equal intervals, but not twelve. One could accomplish the latter feat by addressing select portions of the octave rather than swallowing it whole. For example, eight equal divisions of the minor sixth (from *do* up to *la-flat*) added to four equal divisions of the major third (from *la-flat* to the *do* above it) will do the trick.

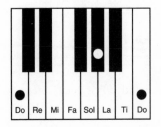

Music theorist Gioseffo Zarlino made matters somewhat easier in 1558 when he described the *mesolabium*, an invention attributed to Archimedes and discussed by Vitruvius in his ninth-century book on architecture. This mechanical device is a measuring tool with diagonal markers that move along strings to find any desired proportion. Zarlino published instructions on how to use the mesolabium for tuning the lute. Other methods included one developed by Philo of Byzantium, who, in the second century B.C.E., used a circle and secant; and another invented in the seventeenth century by Marin Mersenne, who employed intersecting triangles. Of

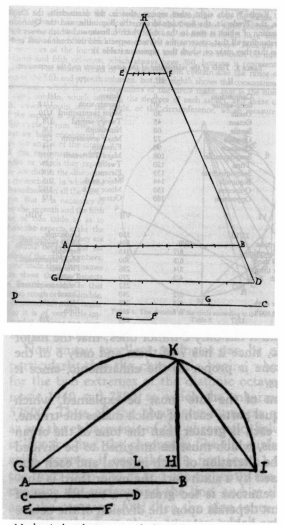

Mechanical solutions to finding the mean of any proportion, from Marin Mersenne's *Harmonie universelle* (1636–37)

course, in a pinch, there was always the equal-temperament tuning method suggested by Giovanni Maria Lanfranco in 1533: Simply tune the fifths flat so "that the ear is not well pleased with them," he said, and the thirds as sharp as one can bear. The result, believed Lanfranco, was close enough.

Discovering that equal temperament was possible did not make it acceptable, however. Indeed, this tuning must have sounded very odd to many of Willaert's contemporaries. It is wondrously free of "wolves," inconsistencies, or unpleasant surprises. To our modern ears, attuned to today's pianos, it is a perfectly beautiful tuning. Yet, its sound was a radical departure at the time. Creating twelve equal steps in an octave changed the proportions that had been used for the various musical intervals, some more drastically than others. Equal-tempered fifths, for example, are closer to pure (3:2) than the fifths used in mean-tone tuning. But major thirds in equal temperament are tempered seven times as much as the fifths. Minor thirds are tempered eight times as much. In the end, these alterations are not intolerable: None of these intervals sounds bad. But in comparison many seem robbed of their original character. This was readily noticed in the sound of equal-tempered major thirds: Lustrous and calm in their pure form, they were now slightly rough and somewhat bland.

What's more, strong ideological objections to equal temperament persisted. Though one prominent composer would bow to Willaert as "the new Prometheus of celestial harmony," critics still compared *Quid non ebrietas* with Archimedes' unsuccessful attempt to square the circle. One reason was the philosophical underpinning of his venture. After all, the formidable authority of Pythagoras was under attack. What's worse, it was being threatened by the ascendance of an ancient rival—Aristoxenus. Willaert had joined the camp of the very renegade philosopher whose third century B.C.E. musings on the possibility of an equal division of the octave had triggered Boethius's blustery dismissal of the idea. Besides, this music was just not easy. According to the composer and theorist Giovanni Spataro, a student of Ramos and choirmaster of Bologna's basilica, *Quid non ebrietas* was in fact performed by the singers of the papal chapel: "but not very successfully."

Willaert's piece was composed in the year Ferdinand Magellan first set sail, and the tenor in *Quid non ebrietas* moves through difficult musical straits like an explorer conquering uncharted regions. However, Willaert's map, unlike those of Columbus or Magellan, was unfailingly clear. His music reflected not so much a venture into the unknown as it did a composer boldly staking a position. Nevertheless, Willaert shared with those seafaring adventurers a quality increasingly prized in an age of spiritual vertigo: *virtù*—prowess.

It was prowess that distinguished the towering mastery of Michelangelo, enabling his individual style to bristle with intensity and drama. Through prowess, artists gained license to pursue a personal vision, forge a new standard, even defy nature—and triumph. Martin Luther's description of composer Josquin des Prez put it succinctly: "He is the master of the notes; others are mastered by them." (There is nothing like that kind of good press. Willaert once discovered the singers of the papal chapel performing one of his own six-part motets; they believed, mistakenly, that it was by Josquin. When they learned the true identity of the composer, they lost all interest in the piece.)

A woodcut of composer Josquin des Prez

Along with painters and composers, musical performers aspired to greater heights of virtuosity and cultivated their skills as improvisers, often peppering the plain melodies they encountered with ornate filigree culled from manuals on the art of embellishment. This, too, could provoke opposition. Josquin, on hearing a singer ornament his music beyond recognition, once flew into a rage. "You ass," he cried. "If you wish to improve on finished compositions, make your own, but leave mine unimproved." Indeed, every advance was cause for conflict. Throughout the sixteenth century, traditional values seemed slowly to crumble, and partisans in nearly every sphere began to cross swords.

The tremors extended even to the disposition of the globe itself. In 1514, the astronomer Copernicus circulated a manuscript among friends in which he made the startling assertion (already proposed by Aristarchus in the third century B.C.E.) that the earth was not at the center of the cosmos. This was later followed by a fuller treatise, *On the Revolutions of the Celestial Spheres.* Copernicus had actually set out merely to restore the ancient tenets of celestial motion by correcting a flaw in the model set out by Ptolemy, in which the planets did not move in a uniform circular motion. Though his revision had little impact at the time (his book was not published until 1543; Copernicus, on his deathbed, saw one of the first copies, smiled, and passed away within the hour), it was yet another step in the collapse of certainty.

. The greatest threat to cultural stability, however, could be found at the church's own door, where, to sustain an increasingly lavish papal lifestyle, redemption was being offered at the auction block. It was an ingenious plan, made propitious by Pope Sixtus IV's proclamation of 1476 announcing the offering of indulgences even for souls already suffering in purgatory. Business soared. One of the policy's most successful peddlers was a Dominican friar named Johann Tetzel, who traveled from town to town guaranteeing swift transport for any human soul to the doors of Paradise. As soon as he heard coins ringing in his bowl, Tetzel proclaimed, those for whom payment was made would fly out of purgatory and straight to heaven. Relatives of the departed scurried to save their loved ones.

Success carried its own dangers, however. In Boccaccio's fourteenth-century literary masterpiece *The Decameron,* a nonbeliever is converted through the argument that Christianity must be divine or it could never have survived the immorality of its clergy (a thought later revisited by Voltaire). Boccaccio's readers could digest that satiric jibe with a knowing smile. But times had changed. Clerical hypocrisy was suddenly more difficult to swallow.

There were calls for reform. Pope Innocent VIII (1484–92) not only ignored them but established a new bureau to bestow favors, and went on to mortgage the papal tiara to pay for the wedding party of his son Franceschetto to an heir of the Medici family. With his successor, Rodrigo Borgia (Pope Alexander VI), whose tawdry exploits with his infamous daughter, Lucrezia, scandalized Europe, the moral fiber of the church unraveled even further. (So did the safety of its wards. The pontiff, who could have a man's tongue torn out and his hand cut off for telling a joke at his expense, apparently made a habit of poisoning his cardinals in order to seize their property.)

All the while, the grand display continued. To celebrate the fall of Granada to Christian forces, Alexander staged a bullfight in the Piazza of Saint Peter. His parties were unparalleled. One of the most notorious was known as the "Ballet of the Chestnuts," an appellation based on the game fifty naked prostitutes performed before invited guests. Little wonder that the great writer Erasmus warned women to keep a distance from "brawny, swill-bellied monks." "Chastity," he wrote, "is more endangered in the cloister than out of it." As Luther nailed his ninety-five refutations of the sale of papal indulgences onto the door of a Wittenberg church on October 31, 1517, conditions were ripe for change.

But change was not always for the better. Denouncing what he saw as the abandonment of faith in favor of clever argument, Luther called for an end to logic. "Reason . . . ," he said, "is the Devil's greatest whore. . . . Throw dung in her face . . . drown her in baptism." Religious sects, germinating across Europe like so many mean-tone tunings, heartily embraced that rallying cry. The new prophets included Andreas Carlstadt (among the first to renounce vows of celibacy by taking a fifteen-year-old girl as his wife), who declared schools and studies the enemies of piety and proclaimed illiterates the only real Christians. Carlstadt banned music as well, because the "lascivious notes of the organ awaken thoughts of the world."

The movement was fertile ground for "mad saints" like Netherlander Jan Beukelsz, an advocate of polygamy who in 1534 discovered a remedy for some of the difficulties inherent in such an arrangement—he had one of his wives murdered. By the end of the century, the most powerful reformer after Luther, French-born John Calvin, had fashioned Geneva into an authoritarian state where freethinking became a crime. Dancing, singing (other than hymns), bells, and even incense were banned. Biblical exegesis assumed the rule of law: A man was jailed for naming his child Claude instead of Abraham; women were punished for their hairstyles; new statutes controlled the color of clothes and the number of dishes at a meal. The penalties were severe: Public burning became one of the few means of entertainment officially sanctioned.

Erasmus, who marveled in 1517 that all over the world, "as

if on a given signal, splendid talents are stirring," formed a drearier evaluation as the epoch wore on. Just before his death in 1536, he called it "the worst age of history." Nevertheless, for many citizens there was much to celebrate.

Fresh resources from across the seas and a strengthening market economy brought a wave of luxury to Europe. Exotica from the New World included tobacco, said to have great medicinal properties, and potatoes, which, because of their testicular shape, were considered an aphrodisiac. (Hence Falstaff's cry, in *The Merry Wives of Windsor,* as he embraces Mistress Ford: "Let the sky rain potatoes!") Many new delights were manufactured closer to home, such as table forks from Venice—promptly condemned by a German preacher, since God would not have given us fingers if he had wished us to use such an instrument—and spoons. (Surprisingly, well into the seventeenth century, opposition to these devices could still be found, even in the highest places. Louis XIV, who was praised for his ability to eat chicken stew with his fingers without spilling a drop, refused to allow the Duke of Burgundy even to display a fork in his presence.)

The first flat plates, produced in Antwerp, appeared at this time, as did the first windowpanes. Handkerchiefs were an especially treasured newcomer. As Erasmus, in his treatise *Civility,* explained: "To wipe the nose on the cap or sleeve belongs to rustics; to wipe the nose on the arm or elbow to pastrycooks; and to wipe the nose with the hand, if by chance at the same instant you hold it to your gown, is not much more civil. But to receive the excreta of the nose with a handkerchief turning slightly away from noble people is an honest thing."

Among the most esteemed accoutrements to the good life were elegantly crafted harpsichords. The instruments were in demand in France, Germany, England, Spain, Italy, and Antwerp—valued as commodities in international trade and as an essential component in the best aristocratic homes, where they were sought as much for their designer cabinetry as for their ability to make music. By the end of the century, Duke Alfonso II of Modena owned fifty-two of them, and he was not alone. Henry VIII set an example for the nobility in England by his artful performances on keyboard instruments (he also played the lute, sang from scores at sight, and composed masses and songs). Ships bound for the Spanish colonies of the New World carried harpsichords among their cargo.

In fact, market competition for the sale of these instruments could be intense, especially between Italian manufacturers and those in Flanders, where famed builders like the Ruckers family, establishing workshops beside a flourishing stock market and diamond industry, proved themselves a force to be reckoned with. (Merchants would often claim for their instruments the country of origin that happened to fetch the highest price at the moment.) In Antwerp, the Guild of Saint Luke for the first time accepted keyboard craftsmen among its members in order to protect them from unwanted competition, just as it had shielded other tradesmen since 1382. The instruments had become economically important enough to warrant such a covenant—and to provoke serious labor disputes as well. One was set off by a French instrument makers' guild in 1520, when the organization claimed the right of its members to decorate their instruments themselves with inlay and marquetry. Furniture makers became so incensed they invaded an organ builder's shop and confiscated all his works in progress.

As these musical instruments grew in prominence, they could become political as well as economic pawns, sometimes with disastrous effects. Henry VIII's desire to dissolve his marriage to Catherine of Aragon and replace her with Anne Boleyn brought an impasse with Rome, so in an Act of Supremacy in 1534, Henry confiscated all lands belonging to the Holy See, founded a new national church, and appointed himself and his successors its head. From that time on, organs, regarded as vestiges of Rome, became a threatened species.

Anti-organ sentiments brought an end to the instrument's ritual role in chapels throughout England. Some were dismantled. The official attitude was summed up in one typical homily given in 1563: "We ought greatly to rejoice and give thanks, that our churches are delivered out of all those things which displeased God so sore, and filthily defiled his holy house and his place of prayer." With the excommunication of Queen Elizabeth in 1570, anti-organ bias turned even more brutal. The queen herself seemed to carry no great animosity toward the instrument—she sent one as a gift to Sultan Mehmet III in Constantinople, complete with an impressive clock and an array of mechanical toys. Nevertheless, for a time, her defenders on the home front happily obliterated every organ from sight. (A century later, the cycle would begin again with a Lords and Commons Ordinance of 1644 calling for "the speedy demolishing of all organs, images and all matters of superstitious monuments in all Cathedrals . . . throughout the kingdom of England and the Dominion of

Wales, the better to accomplish the blessed reformation so happily begun and to remove offences and things illegal in the worship of God.")

Changing ideas about music itself presented a more subtle threat to the future of both organs and harpsichords. Willaert's vocal experiment spawned others directed toward the limitations of the keyboard, like those of avant-garde composer Nicola Vicentino. Vicentino, who described himself as a student of Willaert, was intrigued by the same issues that had gripped Ramos, Ficino, and Pico: What secret had the ancient Greeks possessed that made their music so extraordinarily powerful? Part of the answer, he decided, must lie in subtle tonal shadings that are no longer a part of musical art—unheard notes caught between the keyboard's cracks. He constructed an entirely new instrument, the archicembalo, with *six rows* of keys, to allow different versions of each scale member to be played (commas and all). He wrote a treatise on the ancient styles and provided compositions to demonstrate the point.

This was music that rendered ordinary keyboards helpless. Naturally, these escapades embroiled Vicentino in a passionate dispute, which had to be settled before a musical court in Rome in 1551. The outcome was never in question. Vicentino was too ardently naïve to realize that the deck would be stacked against him from the beginning.

Vicentino hoped to rekindle the ancient fires by freeing music to follow more intricate paths—as it once did, he claimed, for the benefit of "refined ears in praise of great personages and heroes"—instead of the more commonplace ones, "sung in public festivities in public places, for the use of vulgar ears." If his goal carried a hint of elitism, it also attested to a yearning for something deeper, sweeter, better—and more artful. But intricacy was certainly not everyone's ideal. The Vatican, for one, had its own deeply held positions on the subject, as it did about every aspect of life. And by midcentury the institution was readying a comeback.

A counter-reformation was gearing up, and its key word was "piety." A good many believers had been pleading for the change. Around the time of the founding of the Society of Jesus by Ignatius of Loyola in 1540, even fashion throughout Europe began to reflect a new religious sensibility, moving dramatically from low-cut bodices and gold or silver embroidery to the somber black materials prevalent in Spain. (Thankfully, in the next century bright colors from France would again win the day.) The Council of Trent, convened between 1545 and 1563 in an effort to clean house and regain the spiritual high ground, produced decrees on every imaginable subject, from ending the abuse of wealth and privilege to ridding art of its unchaste influences and "superfluous elegance." Of course, the very nature of art had made it a recurring problem. From the removal of Fra Bartolomeo's *Saint Sebastian* from a church because the "women sinned in looking at it for its soft and lascivious imitation of living flesh" to Pope Adrian VI's (unrealized) plan to redecorate the ceiling of the Sistine Chapel in order to cover its naked figures, art was an area that seemed to require constant diligence. The secular bent of Renaissance thinkers only fanned the flames: In 1550 physician and mathematician Girolamo Cardano unabashedly recommended to scholars that they follow a routine of "reading love stories and putting up pictures of beautiful maidens in their bedroom," because "study dissipates the animal spirits."

Music, it seemed, could pose as much of a danger. In 1562, the council urged the exclusion from churches of "all such music as . . . introduces anything of the impure or lascivious, in order that the house of God may truly be seen to be the house of prayer." Luther had praised music of complexity, in which nature is "sharpened and polished by art." In its intricacy, he wrote in 1538, "one begins to see with amazement the great and perfect wisdom of God in His wonderful work of music, where one voice takes a simple part and around it sing three, four, or five other voices, leaping, springing round about, marvelously gracing the simple part, like a square dance in heaven. . . . He who does not find this an inexpressible miracle of the Lord is truly a clod, and is not worthy to be considered a man."

Nevertheless, according to tradition, the Council of Trent was on the verge of banning counterpoint in music altogether when Cardinal Carlo Borromeo of Milan stepped forward. Borromeo was a devout servant of the church who, it was said, sold his furniture to feed the poor, slept on straw, and lived on bread and water. When bubonic plague broke out in August 1576 and many leaders fled, Borromeo, believing it was a punishment from the Almighty, stayed behind; he walked the corpse-ridden streets barefoot with a rope around his neck, carrying a lifesize crucifix—and survived another eight years. Legend has it that Borromeo induced composer Giovanni Pierluigi da Palestrina to write a piece that would convince council members of the efficacy of skillful musical counterpoint in a sacred cause. Palestrina's conservative

style—a combination of luminous clarity and lyrical grace—
did the trick. The composer's restrained approach became
enshrined as the venerable standard by which all future compositions would be judged.

Yet, the ultramodern approaches spearheaded by
Willaert and Vicentino continued to gain adherents; before
the century had ended they gave rise to a music of boundless
extremes. The purveyor of these fantastic sounds was an
eccentric prince and notorious wife-murderer named Carlo
Gesualdo. His story has the makings of a pulp-fiction adventure. At the time of her marriage to Gesualdo, the beautiful
Donna Maria d'Avalos, at twenty-five, had already been wid-
owed three times. The prince—often ill-humored, impetuous, obsessive about music and hunting—could not have
been much of a companion. Donna Maria took a lover;
Gesualdo became suspicious, set a trap, and took revenge. It
changed the course of his life.

The prince had apparently never composed music before
that fateful evening in 1590 when Donna Maria and her lover
succumbed to Gesualdo and his troops. Four years after the
event, however, Count Alfonso Fontanelli, who traveled with
Gesualdo as the composer journeyed to marry yet again—
this time the Duke of Ferrara's daughter—reported that the
prince was showing "his works in score to everybody in order
to induce them to marvel at his art." One night, recalled
Fontanelli, Gesualdo searched for a keyboard so another
member of the party, composer and organist Scipione Stella,
could perform. Finding none, he played the lute for an hour
and a half. Fontanelli's assessment was astute: "It is obvious
that his art is infinite, but it is full of attitudes, and moves in
an extraordinary way." (As for the second marriage, the

result was once again dismal. The new groom often beat his bride, then made a habit of inflicting physical punishment on himself for his transgressions. As the years progressed, the composer's erratic emotions became crippling and he retreated into a psychological shell.)

At the court of Ferrara, Gesualdo and Stella attended a performance played on Nicola Vicentino's multiple-keyboard instrument, the archicembalo. Stella, who apparently had difficulty tuning the archicembalo, was nevertheless taken with its advantages. He later instigated the creation of yet another innovative keyboard: Fabio Colonna's *sambuca,* based on a division of the octave into thirty-one parts. Gesualdo must have recognized in the music he heard on Vicentino's invention the handiwork of a like spirit.

His pieces use bold sounds like those found in Vicentino's musical world, to reflect the stirrings of an anguished soul. The music is by turns tragic, erotic, and shocking. Tortuous melodies squirm and leap uneasily through conventional barriers. Harmonies heave and sigh as they strain to find resolution. Word images are "painted" with hallucinatory effect, causing a line like "to love you or die!" to sag and deflate into a surreal depiction of a life painfully expiring. Gesualdo's texts portray a consuming, incurable passion. They are stories not of love's ultimate fulfillment, but of relentless yearning—of a heart languishing in the fires of unsated desire—and his music captures that state with remarkable potency.

It represented everything the church was hoping to quell.

10

The Alchemy of Sound

It is our fault we love only the skull of Beauty
Without knowing who she was, of what she died.

—Paul Bowles, *scene VI* from *The Thicket of Spring*

Galileo Galilei set a series of pendulums in motion and watched as they swung to and fro. The once lifeless objects, now engaged in a dance of dangling weights, plunged toward the earth, then lifted high again in alternating arcs—creating what the scientist later described as "a beautiful entwining," like invisible wheels of a celestial clock. His pendants had been designed to rise and fall at specific speeds in relation to each other, corresponding to the musical octave (2:1), fifth (3:2), and third (5:4). Through this mechanical ballet, Galileo exclaimed, his eye could see, for the first time, "the same games that the ear hears."

The scene is soaked in symbolism: a harmony of spheres, driven by the unseen governor of the universe, made tangible through beautiful proportion. Yet, Galileo's purpose was anything but mystical. The man who revolutionized astronomy—revealing Jupiter's satellites and Venus's phases, and demonstrating the moon to be nothing but a craggy stone illuminated by reflection—had set these pendants in flight simply for the purpose of analyzing their behavior. Through experiments with pendulums, Galileo discovered a phenomenon known as isochronism—their tendency to keep the time of an oscillation constant even as the energy driving them dwindles (made possible by the fact that as the movement slows the arc grows shorter). From observing pendulums he developed the laws of falling bodies and of objects descending along inclined planes. Along the way, he arrived at a theory of why some musical harmonies are agreeable and others discordant.

The explanation for music's rules of beauty was thoroughly at odds with contemporary thought: as radical as his claim that all bodies, even those of unequal weights, fall to earth at the same speed. For Galileo, accepted opinion meant little. His contemporary the famed astronomer Johannes Kepler eagerly engaged in complex arguments to support the belief that the positions and movements of the planets were calibrated to the just-intonation musical scale. Galileo had his own blind spots: He failed, for example, to adjust his circular model of the planets' orbits even after Kepler discovered that they moved in ellipses, and scoffed at that astronomer's assertion that the moon can exert an influence on the earth's tides. Yet Galileo had no great philosophical axe to grind. While Kepler could assert with confidence that there *must* be life on Jupiter, because it would do no good to have four moons circling the planet without someone there to see them, for Galileo nature never "cares a whit whether her abstruse reasons and methods of operation are understandable to men.

For that reason," he wrote to Christina, the Grand Duchess of Tuscany—defending his discoveries against the objections of some theologians—"it appears that nothing physical which sense-experience sets before our eyes, or which necessary demonstrations prove to us, ought to be called in question (much less condemned). . . ." The concerns of science, he argued, were separate from those of religion. Unfortunately, in the end this argument did little to appease his inquisitors.

Galileo's interest in experimental observation—and, in all likelihood, his curiosity about pendulums—were a legacy of his scientifically inclined musician father, Vincenzo, who was by all accounts as spirited and obstinate a man as his son. Indeed, Vincenzo Galilei's experiments in acoustics, for which he used hanging pendants (inert pendulums) to vary the tensions of vibrating strings, led to one of the greatest feuds in the history of music.

It all began with an apprenticeship. Vincenzo and a band of other musicians, poets, and noblemen regularly met at the home of Florence's influential and colorful Count Giovanni Bardi for the purpose of making music and conversing on art, science, and philosophy. The group, known as the Florentine Camerata, was a hotbed of intellectual activity—"a delightful virtual continuous academy" is the way Bardi's son, Pietro, later recalled it (noting for the historical record that its members kept "vice and every sort of gambling in particular at a distance").

Bardi was the cabal's magnet—a model Renaissance man. He soldiered in the war with Siena, fought against the Turks in Malta, and commanded Tuscan troops in defense of

Emperor Maximilian II in Hungary. Yet he could also improvise a sonnet. On being admitted to the Accademia degli Alterati in 1574, Bardi was cited for his facile command of mathematics, astrology, cosmography, and poetry. "Therefore it is no wonder," stated his anonymous sponsor, that this man, "altogether well proportioned in his soul and body, has always had the greatest affection for the sweet and delightful harmony of music, the art of the ancient Greeks, among whom all the noble arts and virtues flourished to such a degree that whoever was not expert and practiced in it was reputed to be uncouth and worthless."

Like many of his colleagues, Bardi regarded the arts with a sense of gravity befitting their role in what was viewed as the rebirth of civilization. He engaged in the culture wars with the same fervor he displayed against the Turks on the fields of honor, and became embroiled in one of the biggest artistic controversies of the day—whether Ariosto or Tasso was the greater epic poet. (For those still keeping score, Bardi sided with Ariosto.) Until his political fortunes took a bad turn—his endorsement of the marriage of Francesco de' Medici to Bianca Capello had provoked the ire of Ferdinando de' Medici, who, upon his succession in 1587, gave many of Bardi's duties at court, such as control of entertainments and spectacles, to the Roman Emilio de' Cavalieri—Bardi was a fearless mover and shaker in the artistic life of Florence. When he decided to send Vincenzo Galilei to Venice to study under the renowned music theorist Gioseffo Zarlino, however, he could not have predicted the political fallout.

Zarlino was a master musician, a student of logic, Greek,

and Hebrew, and an ordained representative of the church. Born in 1517 on Chioggia, one of the islands in the Venetian lagoon, he received his early training under the tutelage of Franciscan friars, then became a pupil of renowned composer Adrian Willaert. His 1558 book, *Le istitutioni harmoniche,* was a milestone in the history of music theory—an all-encompassing treatise offering the philosophical, mathematical, and practical foundations of musical composition, from the theories of the ancient Greeks to the art of modern harmony.

Within its pages, the author addressed a knotty challenge. Music, believed Zarlino, is a force that can balance body and soul, and bind together the parts of the world; it can do all this because it is a system built on harmonious proportion—the ratios discovered by Pythagoras. Yet, Pythagoras's formulas left no room for some harmonies that had become highly desirable: major thirds, minor thirds, and their upside-down counterparts, sixths. How could this breach between theory and practice be mended?

Zarlino rescued Pythagoras by revising him. According to ancient tenets, the octave (*do* to *do*) is formed by the ratio 2:1; the fifth (*do* to *sol*) by 3:2; the fourth (*do* to *fa*) by 4:3. For Pythagoras the perfection of these musical formulas had been reinforced by the fact that they were built entirely from the first four integers. (When added together, 1, 2, 3, and 4 form the magic number 10—for Pythagoras, a symbol of completeness.) But using only the first four integers leaves out the possibility of forming a major third (*do* to *mi*), whose ratio is 5:4; the major sixth (*do* to *la*), formed through the ratio 5:3; and the minor third (*re* to *fa*), created through the proportion 6:5.

The Alchemy of Sound

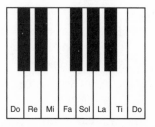

To accommodate these now popular harmonies, Zarlino cleverly expanded the series. Harmony, he explained, could still be divined from the mystical properties of simple numbers. All that was needed was a slight corrective: Musical concords, he asserted, may be formed not only by combinations of the first four integers, but by the first six—a series he called the *senario,* or *sonorous number.*

Like all philosophers searching for a clue to God's great unchanging plan, Zarlino bolstered his position with arguments he believed were stronger than the mere evidence provided by human ears. Six is, he argued, the first "perfect number," being the sum of all the numbers of which it is a multiple (in plain language, $1 + 2 + 3 = 1 \times 2 \times 3$). There are (or so it seemed at the time) six planets in the sky. Plato, in his *Philebus,* indicated that hymns should not celebrate more than six generations. The world was created in six days. And using the first six numbers to form the musical consonances, instead of the first four, solved all of the system's problems—sort of.

Only one kink remained: The proportion that yields a minor sixth (*mi* to the *do* above it) is 8:5—and the number 8 lies outside the first six integers. Yet creating a *senario* that used the entire series of integers up to 8 would have brought disastrous results, since the number 7 generates intervals considered to be harshly dissonant. Zarlino dispensed with the problem by using a typically Aristotelian sleight-of-hand: Although 8 is not *actually* included in the senario, it is there *potentially,* he said. Simply consider it twice 4. Or insinuate it stealthily by joining two other acceptable harmonies: a minor third, *mi* up to *sol;* and a fourth, *sol* up to *do.* This tidy resolution of a thorny predicament satisfied Zarlino and his many followers, including his student Galilei—for a while. On Galilei's return to Florence, however, he experienced a growing sense of dissatisfaction with his teacher's ideas.

W. H. Auden once wrote that man is part eros and part dust. Renaissance scholars like Galilei and Bardi hoped to rekindle eros in their own culture by freeing the ancients from the dust of time. Yet, on closer inspection, Zarlino's musical practices and that of the Greeks seemed worlds apart. The magical secrets of musical art in that ancient civilization were as enticing as ever—and as elusive. In search of more satisfying answers, Galilei and Bardi turned to a man who had devoted his life to understanding the musical treatises of antiquity.

His name was Girolamo Mei, and he could not, he claimed, play, sing, or dance. His manner of dress was old-fashioned, and his long, olive-complexioned face capped by a thatch of black hair, was often adorned with spectacles. Though described by some contemporaries as phlegmatic, he was seen by others as having a "bizarre and lusty humor." Both were probably true. As one of the most respected literary men of Florence, he belonged to the illustrious Accademia Fiorentina, yet he also enjoyed membership in the notorious Pianigiani, a group whose raucous, kabbalistic orgies were halted under pressure from the pope. He seemed always ready to debunk prevailing wisdom. Mei was a singular personality.

He was notorious among the literati for insisting that Florence was not founded by Augustus, as generally believed, but by the less illustrious Desiderio, king of the Longobardi. Duke Cosimo grew angry at the notion. "I never knew how to adapt the intellect to the side opposite of what reason showed me to be true, or to conceal the truth once I have learned it," declared an unrepentant Mei. In the summer of 1561 he began to apply his sharp instincts toward another controversial subject: the nature of ancient music, "about which one reads so many miracles."

Galilei's letter to Mei in 1572 initiated an ongoing correspondence that transformed Zarlino's former student into his fiercest adversary. After long study, Mei had concluded that modern counterpoint—the intricate art of placing one melody against another—so beloved by Zarlino (who had learned its rules from his learned master, Willaert, and which he believed to be a reflection of the heavenly orbs, "turned round their intelligences with harmony"), was actually the reason for music's loss of magic. Only a single melody, uncorrupted by the entanglements of others, could have the ability to arouse a man's affections, asserted Mei. *This,* he said, is how music was performed in the ancient world. Modern practice, Mei argued, produces an overly complex texture, a myriad of musical lines whose individual affects end up working at cross purposes. They nullify each other, so that the end result is no affect at all.

What's more, Mei insisted, Zarlino's cherished just-intonation scale, in which octaves, fifths, and thirds are all based on their pure ratios (2:1, 3:2, and 5:4)—and their supposed sanction by the ancient sage Ptolemy—was a sham. It had been *scorned* rather than praised by the Greeks, he claimed. As to the widely held assertion that singers used this scale naturally, nothing could be further from the truth. To prove his point, Mei challenged Galilei to an experiment: He wanted him to stretch two strings over a lute; under one he was to mark the spots that correspond to the tones produced by Pythagoras's tuning based on perfect fifths, and under the other, the spots that correspond to Zarlino's tuning, based on a combination of perfect fifths and pure thirds. He asked Galilei to play both and compare them to what he actually heard when singers performed.

Galilei mulled over the matter and concluded that *neither* of these scales corresponded to what he was hearing in performance. (A listener today with a good critical ear could reach the same conclusion after listening to a barbershop quartet. These homespun singers, performing in tight formation without the aid of instrumental support, use none of those fixed tunings—or, rather, they alternate between all of them in an ever-shifting search to create agreement between their voices.) From that time on, Galilei's path of discovery would carry him toward a truly radical conclusion: that music must be freed entirely from the tyranny of inviolable number. In 1578 he sent Zarlino an anonymous discourse refuting his former teacher's theories. Two years later, his querulous book on ancient and modern music, *Dialogo della musica antica et della moderna,* was delivered to a printer in Venice. Though Zarlino appears to have used his influence to hold up production, it finally saw the light of day at the end of 1581 or the beginning of 1582. The feud was on.

Galilei's attack hit at everything the older theorist held dear. Just intonation, with its pure fifths and pure thirds, may be an ideal, charged Galilei, but in practice it is a fantasy. Singers continually adjust as they go along, automatically altering the intervals they produce to create beautiful sounds. In any case, the fact is, the human ear easily learns to accept tempered intervals. Indeed, it had already been clearly shown on instruments that equal temperament works wonderfully.

Zarlino was mortified. He recognized the need for applying temperament to some instruments. Lutes were commonly set in equal temperament, because their physical design, which requires several strings to share the same fret, made it necessary; and keyboards were generally set in mean-tone temperament, which altered the fifths away from their pure, 3:2 proportions. But denying that the pure ratios of 3:2 for fifths and 5:4 for thirds was the *natural* foundation of music—of singing!—this was sacrilege.

Galilei's claim was preposterous on its face, he declared, and attempted to refute it by means of philosophical reasoning. If singers continually distorted music's *natural* proportions—the ones found in his six-integer *senario*—then the *true* (heaven-sent) harmonic numbers would always remain a mere *potential*. "And yet we see that God and Nature never do anything in vain. Therefore it is necessary to say that this potential is at some time reduced to action." In other words, God would never sanction a world in which the correct musical proportions were not utilized.

In Zarlino's view, Galilei's brand of musical relativism—his willingness to distort music's true proportions—was not only ridiculous but immoral: an assault on God's plan. Arguing that some sounds displease only because our ears are unaccustomed to them, as Galilei did, "is as much as to say that some bad, tasteless food will seem savory after it has been eaten over a long period," he contended. And to say that *any interval at all* may be sung, whether its ratio is found among the harmonic numbers or not, said Zarlino, is similar to claiming that "since man is capable of both good and evil, it is legitimate for him to commit any infamy and act contrary to good custom and against all that is proper and just."

Galilei, of course, would have none of it. "Among the musical intervals, those contained outside the *senario* are as natural as those within it," he wrote. All scales are, after all, manmade. "Whether we sing the fifth in the 3:2 ratio or not is of no more importance to Nature than that a crow or a raven lives three hundred or four hundred years and a man only fifty or sixty." What's more, he added, "let Zarlino trouble his head about this as much as he wishes."

The debate had reached an impasse, each side sticking to its positions. Yet, the argument was far from over. Between the years of Galilei's *Dialogo* of 1581 and another anti-Zarlino treatise, the *Discorso intorno alle opere de Gioseffo Zarlino* of 1589, new experiments had armed the renegade Galilei with even more formidable ammunition to smash the orthodoxy of his former teacher's number mysticism.

It had long been assumed that Pythagoras, after determining the string lengths for the musical consonances, had applied the same proportions to the weights that hung from those strings—achieving the same results by varying tension instead of length. But Galilei discovered that setting up such weights in the standard Pythagorean proportions won't yield the expected result. The octave is produced by the ratio 2:1 when measuring lengths of strings. When the calculation is based on *weights* attached to strings, however, to achieve the same result, the relative weights must be in the ratio 4:1. When varying string *tension* rather than *length,* the usual proportions have to be squared. Fifths, likewise, are produced by different weights, not in the proportion 3:2, as in string length, but by the ratio 9:4. The proportions used for generating fourths when varying weights is 16:9, not 4:3. Viewed from this new perspective, Zarlino's *sonorous number* (comprised of only the first six integers) was meaningless.

And Galilei had even worse news for Zarlino and his followers. His tests had made it clear that *all* proportions used to produce musical concordances are, in the end, *completely unreliable.* Unless the strings used to create the harmony are made of the same "material, length, thickness, and goodness," they simply won't be in tune with each other. Strings of differing quality, he explained, behave in a way analogous to oil and water. These substances seem alike until they are subjected to heat, at which point their distinct boiling points make the difference between them dramatically clear. Similarly, variables in individual strings cause them to react in different ways, though certain materials make the resulting out-of-tuneness more tolerable. (The gut strings used in lutes, for example, will produce equal-tempered thirds that are more pleasant sounding than the ones produced on strings made of steel.) Since it is impossible to achieve even a true unison in everyday performance, no tuning can be called superior to another; and equal temperament, because of its utility, is clearly better suited to modern music.

Zarlino was resolute. He had heard arguments in favor of equal temperament before—some by his own friend the Reverend Don Girolamo Roselli, who had proposed it as a way to "alleviate all the difficulties of singers, players and composers," since it would allow them to sing or play a scale on whichever of the twelve notes they wished, making a kind of "circular music. . . ." By using this temperament, said Roselli, "all instruments will be able to keep their tuning and be in unison." (Vicentino had even earlier noted the horrible clashes that arose from the common practice of tuning keyboards in mean-tone temperament and fretted instruments in equal temperament.)

What's more, Roselli was not alone. Several scientists had by now also become engaged in the issue, and they were passionately advocating the adoption of a tuning based on the equal division of the octave into twelve parts. One was the brilliant mathematician Giovanni Battista Benedetti, whose work on the acceleration of falling bodies anticipated that of Galileo. (Both had been catalyzed by the same book on the raising of sunken ships, written in 1551 by Niccolò Tartaglia.) After performing experiments on vibrating strings, Benedetti wrote a letter to composer Cirpriano de Rore (another Willaert disciple) around 1585, pointing out that singers or players who managed to maintain the "pure" musical intervals throughout a piece would eventually end up out of tune (an argument already proven by Willaert). To see why, wrote Benedetti, one need only calculate the results of all the commas they would encounter. He gave as indisputable proof an example from a chanson by Rore himself.

The most outspoken proponent of equal temperament on the scientific front, however, was the Dutch engineer Simon Stevin, who was the first experimentalist to test Benedetti's proposition—four years ahead of Galileo—that the speed of a falling object is not governed by its weight. Stevin's treatise on music stood Zarlino's theories on their head. Clearly, he stated, equal temperament is, by all available evidence, the *only natural tuning*. All the others contain so many faults, which generate annoying, disruptive commas, that only a fool would take them to be a product of nature.

The problem, proposed Stevin, began with the Greeks, who mistakenly believed that 3:2 was the real ratio of a perfect fifth, when it is obviously only an approximation. Anyone who multiplies this ratio and realizes that its "circle" of twelve tones produces a last note that is out of tune with the first, yet continues to maintain "that the ratio 3:2 is the actual one, he in truth ignores the essential character of addition and subtraction of ratios." Any such person is stubbornly resisting the plain truth; his position is irrational and absurd.

How had the Greeks made such an error? In part, asserted Stevin, it was because they spoke Greek. Dutch, he claimed, is the only language suited to the science of nature. Therefore, it was easier for him to find nature's true tuning. He did this through a simple mathematical formula.

The octave is produced by a ratio of 2:1 and is comprised of twelve different steps. To find the value of each individual step, one need only find a number that, taken to the power of twelve, will yield a final result of 2/1—that is, the number 2. Therefore, each of the twelve steps that make up the octave can be described mathematically as *the twelfth root of two*. As a number, the twelfth root of two is extremely complex—as far from Zarlino's simple ratios as one can get. But, said Stevin, those who insist on believing in the purity of the simple ratios of old over all aural evidence to the contrary—continuing (like Zarlino) to doubt the viability of equal temperament's more complicated mathematical proportions to produce a sweet fifth or third—they are like the person who proclaims, "The sun may lie, but not the clock." Zarlino kept to his clock; he continued to believe that his simple numbers in their *superparticular ratios* (ratios that take the form $\frac{n+1}{n}$), could not be anything but God's own prescription for beauty.

Paradoxically, at around this time, all across Europe a long-festering discord of another sort between the sun and the clock was finally heading toward resolution. The Julian calendar, through errors that had crept in over several centuries, had drifted out of pace with the rhythm of the heavens, and fixed periods of the year were arriving ten days too soon. In order to correct this, a decision was reached to temper the instruments of time.

Pope Gregory XIII introduced a calendar reform by omitting ten days from the month of October 1582—the fifth was to be counted as the fifteenth—and declaring that all years ending in "00" not divisible by 400 would omit the twenty-ninth day in February. Astronomers like Brahe and Kepler cheered the change. But calls to reason are no match in the human psyche for the potency of numbers, which over time become invested with hopes, dreams, and convictions until they are no longer mere numbers but narratives heavy with meaning. Most of the world met Gregory's announcement with outrage and fear.

The Alchemy of Sound

In Frankfurt am Main and Bristol, people rioted against the pope's attempt to rob them of ten days. Protestants declared it a trick of the Antichrist to impose the will of the devil (Gregory's coat of arms contained a dragon, which was pointed to as further evidence of the plot). Rome's real intent, it was said, was to confuse calculations of the end of the world, so some Christians would be caught unprepared. The reform, it was charged, corrupted the divine plan of the universe.

Denmark, Holland, and Protestant regions in Switzerland and Germany refused to adopt it. The emperor Rudolf II attempted to impose it through a secular decree, wisely refraining from any reference to the pope. But traditions die hard. The new calendar was accepted by the German states only in 1700; by England in 1752; by Sweden in 1753; and by Russia not until 1918.

Adjusting the calendar was, of course, not quite like tempering the divine ratios of music. Gregory's reform was designed to bring manmade instruments back into alignment with the heavens. Imposing equal temperament on music would, according to ancient authority, do the opposite, pulling those instruments further away from divine order. The fifth (the interval from *do* to *sol*), for example, jostled from its elegant simplicity of 3:2 in Pythagorean tuning, would in an equally tempered tuning become unwieldy, almost ungraspable: Instead of the perfectly contained and eminently clear 3:2, equal temperament's version of the fifth is symbolized by the mathematical computation $(\sqrt[12]{2})^{7}$—an irrational number. Simon Stevin, in his *Arithmétique,* claimed "that there are no absurd, irrational, irregular, inexplicable" numbers—that no number can be said to be more beautiful or more divine than another. Yet, few thinkers of his time agreed. For Pythagoras, the mere mention of irrational numbers—and by implication, of an unbounded universe—merited a death sentence. And in the year 1600, the church found itself still very much in agreement with that point of view. This was brought home with brutal definitiveness in the case of Giordano Bruno.

Bruno stands today as an icon of freethinkers, a martyr to the cause of unbridled imagination. The theologian and teacher was executed by church authorities in 1600; among the crimes he stood accused of was his assertion that the universe is infinite, filled with innumerable worlds. The concept defied orthodoxy, as equal temperament did, by refusing to acknowledge a universe circumscribed by numerological borders. In an Aristotelian world, this was mutinous.

Bruno's history suggests additional reasons for a bad end. He was in all probability an antipapal spy operating out of the French embassy in London. He was provocative and indelicate, manic and unpredictable, mercilessly overbearing. What seems to have been his real downfall in the end, however, was an inability to keep his sarcasm in check. The recorded accusations, of course, list none of these.

This rebellious theologian was famous in his time as an expert in memory, for which even France's ineffectual King Henry III sought out his mnemonic methods. When asked, Bruno described his secret in typically mystical terms: "Unless you make yourself equal to God, you cannot understand God: for the like is not intelligible save to the like. Make yourself grow to a greatness beyond measure . . . free yourself from the body; raise yourself above all time, become Eternity." If this description seems obscure (and a touch self-serving), it is not difficult to understand the reaction of the students and faculty of Oxford University when he appeared to address them on the fine points of his philosophy. "Philotheus Jordanus Brunus Nolanus," he began,

> doctor of a more abstruse theology, professor of a purer and more innocuous wisdom, noted in the best academies of Europe, an approved and honorably received philosopher, a stranger nowhere save amongst the barbarous and ignoble, the waker of sleeping souls, tamer of presumptuous and recalcitrant ignorance, proclaimer of a general philanthropy, who does not choose out the Italian more than the Briton, the male more than the female, the mitered head more than the crowned head, the man in the toga more than the armed man, the cowled man more than the man without a cowl, but him who is the more peaceable-minded, the more civilized, the more loyal, the more useful; who regards not the anointed head, the forehead signed with the cross, the washed hands, the circumcised penis, but (where the man may be known by his face) the culture of the mind and soul. Who is hated by the propagators of foolishness and hypocrites, but sought out by the honest and the studious, and whose genius the more noble applaud. . . .

An infuriated audience rioted. One George Abbot was a witness to the proceedings. He later reported that Bruno, a man "with a name longer than his body," had chased after fame by endorsing the opinion of Copernicus that the earth went around while the heavens stood still. "Whereas in truth," wrote Abbot, "it was his own head which rather did run round, and his brains did not stand still."

Temperament

Hauled before the church authorities time and again, Bruno would manage for brief periods to restrain his ferocious spirit just long enough to make an apology; he always went free. At the last, he ended the contest of wills by refusing to recant. "Perchance you who pronounce my sentence are in greater fear than I who receive it," he announced, and for his trouble was burned alive at the stake.

Vincenzo Galilei's stance on musical tunings veered perilously close to Bruno's admonition to the poets: Throw off the yoke of authority, he told them; there are no rules other than the ones you make.

Vincenzo's son, Galileo, shared similar ideas, and had the same difficulty in adhering to official doctrine. "I do not feel obliged to believe that that same God who has endowed us with sense, reason, and intellect has intended us to forgo their use," he once stated. By the end of his life, however, he found himself kneeling before the Roman authorities dressed in white penitent's robes and, under command of the Holy Office, renouncing Copernicus's teaching that the earth revolves around the sun.

Science and music had by now joined hands to walk along a single path. Galileo's views on the latter, however, placed him on safer ground, where the transgressions were more subtle and less damaging to pontifical authority. Nevertheless, they still provoked. Bruno had run up against the church in declaring the universe infinite; Vincenzo Galilei had run up against Zarlino in proposing a musical universe of infinite number. If his father was correct in saying that scales are manmade and not a product of Zarlino's magic numbers, asked Galileo, why do the heavens seem to smile on certain combinations of tones and frown on others? Surely, he thought, there is a scientific explanation. Hence he set out to develop a theory of consonance, and formed it while observing his tremulous pendulums. Once again, however, fellow scientist and equal-temperament advocate Giovanni Battista Benedetti had been there first.

Benedetti's theory was as follows. Since the octave is produced by two strings vibrating in the ratio 2:1, the pulses issuing from the higher string and the ones from the lower one will meet in agreement every second time. As the ratios producing various harmonies become more complex, however, they create pulses that meet less and less often. Therefore they sound less consonant. So, despite the claims of Pythagoras and Zarlino, claimed Benedetti, there is no fixed set of harmonious ratios: Dissonance occurs on a sliding scale.

Galileo built on this argument. Take two vibrating strings in the proportion 3:2, he explained. Their pulses will begin simultaneously, followed by a pulse from the upper string, then one from the lower, then another from the upper before the pattern repeats with both strings emitting a sound together again. (Beating a rhythmic pattern of 3 beats in one hand against 2 in the other on a tabletop will illustrate his point.) As musical ratios yield more chaotic patterns, the sounds become more disagreeable, keeping "the eardrum in perpetual torment, bending it in two different directions in order to yield to the ever-discordant impulses": dissonance.

In keeping with the Galilei family tradition, the aesthetic principles he gleaned from this theory were used to deliver yet another swipe at Zarlino's increasingly shaky edifice. The octave, announced Galileo, is not a wondrous sound at all, but an insipid one, because 2:1 is a boring rhythm. The harmony of a fifth, on the other hand, in its complexity, pro-

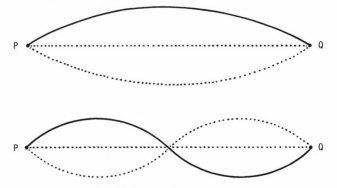

Two strings vibrating in the proportion 2:1. They arrive together at the same position (find agreement) every time the faster one has completed two *pulses,* or excursions away from the center.

duces an interesting mix of "a sweetness with a dash of sharpness."

There were fatal flaws in this theory of consonance. If it were correct, two strings would sound in harmony only if they began at exactly the same instant—otherwise their alternating pulses would never manage to meet. Everyday experience shows that this is not the case (which is why Newton dismissed the notion outright).

There is another weakness as well: The pulses of strings producing the complex ratio of an equal-tempered fifth, even if they were to begin at the same time, will *never again coincide.* Yet, an equal-tempered fifth sounds *less* discordant than a half-step (such as a combination of the tones *mi* and *fa*), in which the pulses of the two tones *do* meet every fifteen pulses. This was one hypothesis that simply didn't work.

However, an alternate theory was in the wings, penned by Kepler, whose three laws of planetary motion forever recast man's view of the solar system. His scheme of a harmonious universe united science, math, music, and religious doctrine into a fantastical—and conceptually breathtaking—defense of Zarlino's precepts.

From his earliest days, mathematical patterns in nature, especially those he could discern in the skies, held a special fascination for Kepler. Childhood smallpox had ravaged his eyes, but "the floor of heaven," as Shakespeare put it in *The Merchant of Venice,* "thick inlaid with patinas of bright gold," illuminated a wondrous vision within him. Through science he believed he would prove true the Bard's poetic account of that ascendant plane: "There's not the smallest orb which thou behold'st / But in his motion like an angel sings. . . ."

"Such harmony is in immortal souls," claimed Shakespeare. "But whilst this muddy vesture of decay / Doth grossly close it in, we cannot hear it." Kepler longed to record this music of the spheres, an obsession begun while he was attending school in Tübingen, where Michael Maestlin, a teacher of Ptolemaic astronomy, secretly instructed him in Copernican theory. From Maestlin he adopted Copernicus's view that the sun, at the center of the universe, "as if seated upon a royal throne, rules the family of the planets as they circle around him." But plenty of questions remained unanswered. Why, he wondered, are there just six planets instead of twenty or a hundred? Why does the sun, floating above the horizon, appear to take up 1/720 of a circle? And to what end does the zodiac divide the sky into twelve parts? The answers came in fits and starts.

They began to appear while he was teaching a geometry class in July 1595. Drawing a figure on a blackboard—a triangle inscribed within a circle, in the center of which there was yet another inscribed circle—he experienced a sudden flash of insight. The ratio between the two circles seemed the same as that between the orbits of Saturn and Jupiter. Could other geometrical figures represent the distances between Jupiter and Mars, Mars and Earth, and so on? Using the five Platonic solids—three-dimensional figures for which all sides are completely symmetrical—he managed to complete the puzzle. (Euclid catalogued these as the pyramid, the cube, the eight-faced octahedron, the dodecahedron—made of twelve pentagons—and the icosahedron, comprised of twenty equilateral triangles.) Incredibly, each one seemed perfectly shaped to fill a particular slot among the five recesses between the floating heavenly spheres. The revelation was a first step in what Kepler described as his ascent "through the harmonic ladder of celestial movements . . . where the true Archetype of the world's structure lies hidden." God's celestial plan, he was now convinced, would be revealed through geometry. With a little searching, he even managed to find the formulas for musical consonance in the proportions created by regular geometric polygons inscribed within a circle.

However, Kepler's wavering personal fortunes gave rise to a rootless life. Forced, with all Protestants, to leave Graz, Austria, he abandoned teaching and found employment as an assistant to the famed (and difficult) astronomer Tycho Brahe. Next he worked for the mad Holy Roman Emperor Rudolf II as chief astronomer of the Imperial Court, fulfilling his duties as the emperor's astrologer. Then tragedy piled on tragedy: He suffered the loss of his first wife to typhus and his daughter to smallpox; at Rudolf's death he was excommunicated by the Lutheran authorities for his ideas. Soon after he was called to his mother's side to defend her against charges of witchcraft (she endured thirteen months of imprisonment before being released, but died shortly after returning home). Yet, he kept working. Upon Brahe's death he was bequeathed all of the astronomer's data (though none of the instruments used to collect it), and Kepler was determined to make the most of it. His skill, in any case, had never rested in gathering information, but in creating and testing hypotheses based on what others had found.

He plotted the orbit of Mars—trying seventy different premises over four years—and concluded that it was not a perfect circle, as every philosopher, theologian, and scientist had long assumed, but an ellipse. (Even Copernicus had claimed that the circle was the most natural course for every planet, since it "does not need any joint. . . . All objects strive to be bounded in this way. This is seen in drops of water and other liquids when they wish to be bounded by themselves.") When he found that the other planets followed elliptical paths as well, it became one of the most momentous scientific discoveries of all time.

For Kepler, this was the missing key. Elliptical orbits revolving around a stationary sun will result in variations in a planet's speed as it hurtles through space. Viewed from the sun's position, for example, Saturn would be perceived to move through an arc of 135 seconds per day when closest, but only 106 seconds when farthest away. Place these two numbers in a proportion (135:106) and the result will be roughly 5:4, the ratio that, when formed between two vibrating strings, produces a pure major third. What happens when Jupiter's proportion is calculated? It generates a minor third. Mars's numbers result in a perfect fifth. Each of the planets,

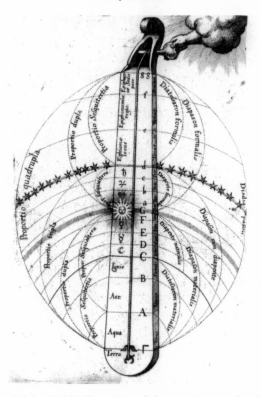

Robert Fludd's illustration of the cosmic monochord
from his *History of the Macrocosm and Microcosm* (1617):
The hand of God tunes the world.

when examined in this way, yields a musical proportion.
God's universe, it seemed, was secretly governed by the just-
intonation musical scale.

During his journey to save his mother from the stake,
Kepler read Galilei on music and rejected him as "ruinous."
If polyphonic (many-voiced) music was unknown to the

ancients, he proposed, it means only that man—"the ape of his creator"—has just now evolved to a stage in which he might finally "to some extent taste the satisfaction of God the workman. . . ." For Kepler, the answers to music's great questions could be found in the firmament—not, as theorist Abraham Bartolus had suggested in his *Musica mathematica* of 1614, by linking musical effects and keys to a composer's horoscope, but by realizing the divine geometry in the mind of God. "Follow me, modern musicians," he entreated. "By your symphonies of various voices, and whispering through your ears, she has revealed her very self, as she exists in her deepest recesses, to the mind of man, the most beloved daughter of God the Creator." For "the movements of the heavens are nothing except a certain everlasting polyphony."

Was this the final answer? Had Kepler uncovered God's true harmonic plan for music and the universe? As seventeenth-century science grew beyond its infancy, and the seeds of a soaring, disquieting musical art flowered to new heights, the debate would continue.

11

A Short Trip to China

With thud of the deep drum,
flutes clear, doubling over all,
concord evens it all, built on
the stone's tone under it all.
T'ang's might is terrible
with a sound as clear and sane
as wind over grain.

—Ezra Pound, *Shih-Ching: The
Classic Anthology Defined by Confucius*

The age of science took its first
small steps through the swinging pendulums, whirling planets, and humming strings of Galilei, Stevin, Benedetti, and Kepler, and before long investigators everywhere were detailing God's hidden handiwork with triumphant satisfaction. On high, the celestial orbs in their elliptical patterns dutifully obeyed Kepler's laws. In the world below, William Harvey, discarding the faulty medical model in use since the second century, revealed the body's true circulatory system. And

A Short Trip to China

William Gilbert, physician to Elizabeth I, built upon the discoveries of seafaring navigator Robert Norman and confidently plotted the behavior of the compass to establish the earth's own invisible sphere of power—the magnetic field, or *orbis virtutis,* a force "exalted above the bounds of corporeal matter." As twentieth-century artist Georges Braque would later declare, art disturbs, but science reassures.

Yet, at the turn of the seventeenth century, the two disciplines in Braque's equation were still closely joined. Laying bare the anatomy of heaven did little to resolve disquieting issues about the nature of beauty and the meaning of art. To further complicate the matter, the aims of artists seemed at that very moment to be shifting dramatically.

As the spirit of experiment grew in science, it seeped into creative activities as well, fostering a virtual explosion of innovation. Between 1580 and 1623, almost eleven thousand new words were added to the English language. (By 1628, Robert Burton, author of the best-selling *Anatomy of Melancholy,* was complaining about the unrelenting flood of new books: "We are oppressed with them, our eyes ache with reading, our fingers with turning.") Diderot's great eighteenth-century encyclopedia labeled this era's building style as "baroque," meaning it was exaggerated and bizarre, and the label stretched to envelop every expressive medium of the age.

Architecture, as well as music, was now concerned with brilliant exhibition and "affect"—not only in representing passions but in agitating them. Composer Claudio Monteverdi, a leader in the new musical practices of the time, was heavily criticized for using unlawful harmonies, "licentious modulations," and "mountainous collections of cacophonies"; today we recognize among his output some of the first great operas.

Scientists trained their focus on these developments and ventured some analytical observations. Kepler applied his mathematical acumen to the issue of music's ability to represent human emotion; among his conclusions was the proposition that major thirds are inherently masculine and minor thirds feminine. When singing *do-re-mi* (encompassing the distance of a major third, from *do* to *mi*), he claimed, one feels the urge to continue and leap up to the next scale tone, *fa*. Clearly, asserted Kepler, the note *mi*, that major third above *do*, is "active and full of efforts"; in his view, the action of reaching from *mi* up to *fa* simulated a male ejaculation. Singing the minor third, on the other hand—the distance between *re* and *fa*, sounded when rendering the notes *re-mi-fa*—induces a desire to fall back down to *mi*. Thus, he proclaimed, the minor third is passive; it tends to sink toward the ground like a hen preparing to be mounted by a cock.

Other, less salty descriptions of these effects had been circulating for some time. The radical composer and inventor of the multi-keyboard archicembalo, Vicentino, who in 1550 described the minor third as "feeble" and "rather sad," also concluded that it liked to descend; in contrast, the major third, he said, preferred to rise "because of its liveliness." Yet, there was far from universal agreement on the subject. The great Elizabethan composer Thomas Tallis composed a series of eight pieces in 1568, each based on the "ethos" of a particular musical scale—one was meek, another sad, yet another filled with rage. But Vincenzo Galilei proclaimed that a *single* interval within a scale may play *dual* roles: The fifth, he said, is sad when ascending, but joyous when falling.

A Short Trip to China

Agreement or not, composers were now vigorously pursuing efforts to expand the emotional impact of their musical works. In a letter to a friend, Galileo offered as good a description as any of the emerging philosophy, which placed an especially high value on ingenuity in instrumental performance. "The farther removed the means of imitation are from the thing to be imitated, the more worthy of admiration the imitation will be," he wrote.

> Will we not admire a musician who moves us to sympathy with a lover by representing his sorrows and passions in song much more than if he were to do it by sobs? And this is so because song is a medium not only different from, but opposite to the expression of pain, while tears and sobs are very similar to it. And we would admire him even more if he were to do it silently, on an instrument only, by means of dissonances and passionate musical accents; for the inanimate strings are less capable of awakening the hidden passions in our soul than is the voice that narrates them.

With this in mind, many keyboard composers pushed the musical language to new frontiers. One was Giovanni di Macque, who had been brought to Naples by Gesualdo's father, Prince Fabrizio Gesualdo da Venosa (and fled in the aftermath of the infamous double murder). Another was Girolamo Frescobaldi, a masterful composer and keyboardist who, according to legend, played the great organ at Saint Peter's before a crowd of thirty thousand. As a boy, Frescobaldi studied in Ferrara under the man cited by Gesualdo as *his* greatest influence, organist Luzzasco Luzzaschi. Even while a youngster Frescobaldi was recognized as a compelling virtuoso. His boldly personal keyboard statements were studies in musical acrobatics, replete with lyrical somersaults, twirling filigree, and impetuous plunges through mazes of shifting moods. Frescobaldi's student Johann Jacob Froberger continued his teacher's tradition; Froberger's own highly individual and passionate style has been preserved in deeply felt works like the *Lament on the Most Grievous Decease of His Imperial Majesty Ferdinand the Third*.

The stretching of musical boundaries fueled a demand for more versatility from the keyboard instruments themselves. While Kepler's introduction of elliptical orbits caused perfect circles to fall from grace in the skies, they were becoming ever more important in the musical realms below. Composers like Frescobaldi wanted a uniformly symmetrical tuning—one built from equidistant steps—with the promise of achieving a graceful circle through all twelve musical notes, reaching from *do* to *do* without the jarring gaps that rendered some keys unusable. However, *physically* dividing the octave into twelve equal parts still remained a challenge—a difficulty overcome on the lute through a formula suggested by Vincenzo Galilei.

Lute frets are placed straight across all six strings on the instrument. When *do-sharp* (on the keyboard, the black note to the right of *do*) is sounded on one string, and *re-flat* (the black note to the left of *re*) on another, it is imperative that they form a true octave. But to accomplish this, the frets have to be spaced apart according to a uniform formula that will insure that after twelve steps are traversed a player will have reached the span of an octave. Galilei considered the old problem of dividing a whole tone (in the proportion 9:8) into two smaller tones (17:16 and 18:17) and proposed that 18:17 be used as a measure for the placement of lute frets. He found that the alternative of 17:16 would result in too few frets; 19:18 in too many. With variances in tension, materials, and finger pressure, using 18:17, claimed Galilei, would produce the most musically satisfying outcome. His formula was almost universally adopted. (Zarlino, of course, found Galilei's reasoning on this—as on everything musical—fallacious.)

In the music history books, however, neither Galilei with his experimenter's savvy nor Stevin with his mathematical brilliance is credited as the originator of a system for equal-temperament tuning. That honor is usually reserved for Prince Chu Tsai-yü, a sixth-generation descendant of Hung Hsi, the fourth emperor of the Ming dynasty. This is a curious circumstance, since Chinese music contained none of the elements that had forced Western musicians toward the use of temperament: no harmonic complexity pitting thirds against octaves and fifths, no crying need to compromise the purity of any musical intervals. And if Chu Tsai-yü's formulas for equal temperament make for a peculiar entry in the textbooks, the origins of his work render them stranger still.

In Western eyes the ways of the East have always been impenetrable. European impressions of those distant lands were shaped early on by amazing tales of Alexander's journeys there. He was said to have encountered Amazons, dog-headed men called Cynocephali, and, odder still, Sciopods—one-legged beings who ran like the wind and then, when resting, used their enormous foot as a sunshade. Beyond the boundaries of Europe, it was once believed, lived unicorns and dragons, serpents with feet, and Mantikhoras—creatures made up of the body of a lion and the face of a man.

Over the centuries, a more faithful picture began to take

shape through sporadic contacts. Ninth-century sailings to Canton from the Persian Gulf enabled Arab geographers to develop more accurate maps. And in the mid–thirteenth century, Genghis Khan's son and successor, Ögödei, presented even greater opportunities for interchange: He invaded Europe. Pope Innocent IV reacted at the time by sending diplomatic letters to "the King and people of the Tartars," using groups of friars as his messengers. (Among the Mongols, one tribe went by the name Tatar; Europeans changed this to Tartar—believing the hordes to have come from Tartarus, the infernal regions—and applied the appellation to the entire race.) A paunchy, middle-aged Franciscan named Giovanni di Pian di Carpine miraculously reached the camp of Batu, khan of the Golden Horde, and managed to deliver the pope's documents. The khan was unimpressed, however: He promptly demanded the pontiff's immediate appearance and submission.

Nevertheless, missionaries and merchants continued to pursue the hidden continent. The most famous was Marco Polo, whose book offered intimate behind-the-scenes glimpses of China's culture. Polo's portrait was not always flattering. He related with horror that in this strange land it was the habit for men to keep up to thirty wives; what's worse, they occasionally offered one to a visitor. "They do not hold as sinful what we hold as very great sins," Polo wrote, "for they live like beasts." In any event, China's exotic lure continued to linger in the European imagination. By 1461, even a pope—Pius II—labored to produce a book about it. Both Pius's *Asia* and Marco Polo's accounts ended up among Columbus's personal belongings.

By the turn of the seventeenth century, a more flattering

picture was emerging. "Who ever expected such wit, such government in China?" Joseph Hall pondered in his 1608 report *The Discovery of a New World*. "We thought learning had dwelled in our part of the world; they laugh at us for it, and well may, avouching that they of all the earth are two-eyed men, the Egyptians the one-eyed, and all the world else, stark blind." This was Chu Tsai-yü's nation, at a time when the doors between the two halves of the world were finally edging open.

Yet, there is nothing to suggest that Chu knew much of the West or of its music. Born in 1536 in Ho-nei, China, he lived an austere life, working under the shadow of a father whose views about the importance of humility and right living caused distress at the imperial court. The elder Chu, known as Chu Hou-huan, was a model of Confucian piety; he wore simple cotton clothes, maintained a vegetarian diet, and was vocal about the need for moral reform. In 1550, the emperor used trumped-up charges of treason to deprive him of his rank and sent him to prison, where he remained for nineteen years. His son, Tsai-yü, left the family ancestral home in protest, built a mud hut outside the palace gate, and began spending all his days inside, studying the subjects his father had pursued: mathematics, astronomy, the science of calendars, and music theory. He was fourteen years old at the time.

Musical tuning in China had a long theoretical tradition with measurements based on bamboo pitch pipes, and Chu became immersed in its intricacies. He went back to the writings of philosopher Huai Nan Tzu in 122 B.C.E. and of Ching Fan, a diviner, astronomer, and mathematician who lived around 45 B.C.E. He studied glosses on their works by Ch'eng-t'ien in the fourth century and Ch'ien Lo-chich, the royal astronomer of the Liu Sung dynasty, in the fifth. Over all these centuries, Chinese scholars had struggled with the challenge of establishing a standard pitch—a tone they referred to as the "Yellow Bell"—and deliberated over the mathematical complexities involved in calculating the eleven tones that should rise above it. The twelve tones used to fill out a full octave were known as *lüs*—the word means law, order, or principle—and efforts to codify them go back to 2700 B.C.E.

The task of determining the right formulas for these tones is made all the more difficult when the instruments being used are bamboo flutes. Musical notes created by blowing into a flute vary not only by the length of the bamboo, but also with the shape of the instrument and its openings, the strength of breath flowing through it, the temperature of the air around it, and other properties peculiar to vibrating pipes. Nevertheless, attempts to establish the mathematics of a proper musical scale continued to evolve with each successive generation. Then, Chu Tsai-yü brought the controversy to a close. "One dawn I had a perfect understanding [of the matter]," reported Chou. He had, he claimed, realized a missing piece of the puzzle: "Something which pitch-pipe exponents had not been conscious of for a period of two thousand years. . . ."

He published his finding in a 1584 treatise called *A New Account of the Science of the Pitch Pipes,* offering a new calculation for dividing the octave into twelve equal parts. He credited the ancient master Huai Nan Tzu with the solution; it had, Chu insisted, been in the work of that great sage all along. Not surprisingly, one cannot find it there. It was typical in Chu Tsai-yü's culture to venerate the ancients even when revising them. Whether or not Chu truly traced his answer to a source in the Han dynasty of 122 B.C.E. does not, however, alter one mystifying question: Why for centuries had Chinese scientists concerned themselves with the problem at all? There was no clear musical need to address it, and the tuning of bamboo pitch pipes was in any case too unreliable in practice to warrant a reckoning of great mathematical subtlety.

The clue to this mystery may lie in the character of the man cited by Chu as the originator of the equal-temperament formula. Known during his life as Liu An, king of Huai Nan, he issued, in addition to these musical propositions, an important Taoist philosophical tract with which he has forever become identified: the *Huai Nan Tzu* (*The Book of Master Huai Nan,* or *The Radiant Light of Huai Nan*).

Taoist tradition teaches that the universe began as an undifferentiated whole—formless, changeless, and eternal—before giving birth to the ten thousand things of this world. The shards of that divine ground of being are all around us, engaged in an endless dance of yin and yang—of female and male, darkness and light, earth and heaven, fullness and emptiness; they seek a harmony of opposites, a fleeting balance, in every moment. Man can fulfill his place in the natural order by finding a resonance with the vital force behind the dance; it's called the Tao—"the Way." And through ritual and music, he can uncover the hidden connections that sustain and unify. Thus, when a lute player strikes the note *kung* on one instrument, says the *Huai Nan Tzu,* the same note will ring on another lute some distance away.

Yet, there is another kind of music, says the text: darkly mysterious and extremely subtle—a sound that can set not just one string of the lute vibrating in sympathy, but all twenty. This is the supreme harmony. The man who sinks into its depths, who "drifts about in its midst in sweet contentment," becomes as one who "had not yet begun to emerge from his origin. This is called the Great Merging." The soul who accomplishes this joins in sympathetic vibration with everything. Huai Nan Tzu was said to be just such a man. He gathered the best Taoist masters of the secret arts to his court. In some accounts, he kept company with the Eight Immortals, from whom he obtained the Elixir of Life. (One story relates how, as he and the Immortals mounted a cloud and began sailing to heaven after drinking the Elixir, Huai accidentally dropped the bottle with this magic potion; his dogs and farm animals licked the remains and sailed up after him.) Among these immortals were Chung-li K'uan, who discovered the magical Elixir; and Chung Kwoh-lao, who had a mule he could fold up like a piece of paper and keep in his wallet. Another was Ho Hsein-Ku, also known as the Immortal Maiden; her symbol was the lotus, flower of openheartedness. And there was Han Hsang-tzu, who had the power to make flowers grow before the eyes of onlookers; Han was the patron saint of musicians, symbolized by the flute—the instrument through which Taoist tradition and musical temperament ultimately meet.

The most plausible explanation for the Chinese interest in equal temperament begins in ancient Taoist ritual, with ceremonies linked to the passing stages of the year. One of these ceremonies was called "waiting for the emanations." Chinese months are more than markers; they each have a specific character—demanding certain modes of behavior, as well as special clothing, colors, and foods. And each month has its proper musical pitch, determined by a bamboo flute—or pitch pipe—of a certain length. As the pages of the calendar turn, the earth itself undergoes changes, both on its natural surface and in the balance of divine energies from above and below which wax and wane through an annual cycle. In the ritual of the emanations, all of these visible and invisible components of a transforming world converge. The earth is made level, and twelve bamboo pitch pipes, filled with ashes, are buried so that their tops are on an even plane. Since they are of differing lengths, the depths to which they sink vary. At the arrival of the first month, the energy rising from the ground reaches the longest pipe and causes its ashes to blow out of the top. At the next month, the emanation reaches the second pipe and scatters its ashes—and so on, until the cycle is complete.

Finding the proper lengths of these pipes is critical. The first and thirteenth notes share the same name, framing the musical scale that will unfold over the course of a year. Between these, the lengths of the flutes that fall between the first and last should graduate in even increments. Thus cut to the correct size, they will produce the proper tones for each month. Among these will be such notable tones as *shang,* which sounds like the bleating of a sheep; and *chüeh,* which resembles the cry of a pheasant; *chih,* like the squeal of a pig; and *yü,* like the neighing of a horse. With all twelve tones in place, the yearly cycle can be completed.

By Chu Tsai-yü's time, this ancient ritual was no longer important; in the eyes of most of his contemporaries, it was hardly credible. Yet, from these Taoist beginnings a mathematical challenge had begun: to construct a division of the octave into twelve equal parts. Through the ages, the problem clearly took on a life of its own, generating over a thousand years of mathematical pursuit. Chu capped the cumulative results of this tradition with a creative solution: extending the old calculations, and offering an elegantly practical new way to create an equal-temperament scale—one akin to Galilei's solution on the lute.

He found his practical answer in the number 749. Scholars in both the East and the West realized that a string of pure fifths, produced by vibrations in the ratio 3:2, will never perfectly close the musical circle, and they each tried to find a way to remedy the problem. Westerners selected one of these fifths to be altered as a sacrificial "wolf," until the solution of equal temperament came along. Chu Tsai-yü's version of temperament was elegant in its simplicity. Through simple multiplication he transformed the proportion 3:2 into 750:500. Using this as his starting point, he then substituted 749 for 750. The resulting fifths (749:500), when stacked in a series of twelve tones (representing twelve monthly gradations), create a nearly perfect equal-tempered circle in which the first and thirteenth tones closely match.

The proportion 749:500 as a guide for producing the interval of a fifth was actually of no practical value in the tuning of bamboo pitch pipes. Nevertheless, the formula marked an important point in a long pursuit. The sages of China, like those of the ancient West, hoped that the mathematics of music would lead them to a connection with the divine. For Huai Nan Tzu, the goal was a resonance with the imperceptible core of life: an essence capable of enlivening earth's gardens and shaping the starry sky, just as it might infuse our minds and open our hearts. Like a Pythagoras of the East, he yoked his quest to the instrument of number. Nearly two thousand years later, his disciple Chu Tsai-yü completed the task.

12

The Scientists Confer

Such sweet compulsion doth in music lie,
To lull the daughters of Necessity,
And keep unsteady Nature to her law . . .

—John Milton, "Arcades"

René Descartes had a tin ear. The preeminent philosopher of the early seventeenth century confessed that he couldn't hear the difference between the sounds of a fifth and an octave, or judge whether someone had sung a scale correctly. He couldn't sing one himself. These deficiencies apparently posed no obstacle for an incisive mind bloated by pride, however, even when passing judgment on the most challenging musical issue of the day. Descartes confidently declared, with the same steely tone of authority used to announce the dynamics of planetary motion or the origin of the tides, that equal temperament's altered proportions were a violation of nature. (Of course, Newton would soon prove him wrong on the behavior of both the planets and the oceans.)

Temperament

Surprisingly, Descartes's earliest treatise was on the subject for which he seemed so ill suited. His *Compendium of Music* was written in 1618 while he was serving in the army of Maurice of Nassau in opposition to the Spanish forces of Ambrogio, marquis of Spinola. Political strife, fueled by religious hatred and a hunger for land, would soon engulf Europe in a devastating thirty-year war. Descartes, for unexplained reasons, had placed himself on the front lines. From a modern perspective, the entire conflict appears to have been sustained for no better reason than the one given by a soldier in Bertolt Brecht's drama about the fight, *Mother Courage:* "Peace is one big waste of equipment." Nevertheless, as hostilities heightened, the philosopher continued a part in the adventure by next joining the forces of Maximilian, duke of Bavaria.

It was while stationed with Maurice near Breda that Descartes met, among the various civilian experts who visited the camp, mathematician Isaac Beeckman, principal of the College of Dort. The two formed an almost instant bond. Beeckman was, Descartes wrote, "the only one to have excited me in my laziness, to have recalled the knowledge that had already virtually disappeared from my memory, and to have guided my mind that was wandering away from serious occupations back towards better things." Their long discussions included a good deal about music, and as the New Year approached and they prepared to part, Descartes wrote the *Compendium* and offered it to his newfound friend as a remembrance. Neither suspected it would one day become the centerpiece of an ugly and protracted dispute between them.

That would occur many years later, when Beeckman,

who kept scrupulous records of their encounters in a diary, suggested that some of his ideas had found their way into Descartes's little musical treatise. The claim sent Descartes into a rage; he denounced his former companion's "empty bragging," his "odious . . . most odious . . . very odious" conduct. He had learned no more from Beeckman, declared the philosopher, than he learns by observing ants and worms. In a 1630 letter, Descartes—after explaining that he never paid attention to *anyone's* opinions, because people so often base their ideas on false principles—adopted a more compassionate tone: Beeckman was not malicious, he said, just sick. (Incredibly, within a year of this fracas the two would meet for lunch.)

Very shortly after leaving Breda, Descartes experienced a famous moment of spiritual and intellectual awakening. According to his own account, he shut himself up in a "stove" to escape the cold in Maximilian's camp (perhaps a room with a stove—the meaning is unclear), fell asleep, and was jolted by three startling dreams filled with light and thunder. He awoke with a sudden revelation: that by applying a mathematical method to philosophy all knowledge of the world could be synthesized into a unified system. Overwhelmed with gratitude for the insight, Descartes pledged a pilgrimage to the shrine of the Lady of Loreto in Italy; within a few months he would, at the age of twenty-three, create analytic geometry.

Though the musical treatise was written prior to this life-altering event, and well before Descartes's ideas had coalesced into the powerfully influential philosophy known as Cartesianism—the view that in this great clockwork of a universe, truth can be grasped through pure reason rather than by a reliance on subjective sense impressions—a suggestion of his later inclinations is already present in this first work. Here, the thinker who will one day propose that the entire world is nothing but a machine—that even human emotions follow mechanical paths—ascribes music's basis to simple, predestined mathematical formulas. For Descartes, human *reactions* to music are subjective; they vary according to circumstance. But musical *science* is objective: Its laws spring from the grinding of nature's wheels, irrespective of capricious human judgment. They exert a truth beyond mere sensation.

He offered some observations on music's emotive powers, nevertheless. The human voice is the most pleasing instrument, he said, because it is the most directly attuned to our souls. "By the same token, the voice of a close friend is more agreeable than the voice of an enemy because of sympathy or antipathy of feelings—just as it is said that a sheepskin stretched over a drum will not give forth any sound when struck if a wolf's hide on another drum is sounding at the same time." Clearly, experimental observation played no part in *that* particular formulation.

The behavior of sheep, wolves, and the human heart notwithstanding, Descartes held fast to his assertion that musical rules are not about what is perceived as beautiful or enjoyable, but about unchanging principles that rise above ephemeral experience. More than a decade after composing the *Compendium,* Descartes cautioned his friend and confidant Father Marin Mersenne—the chief correspondent of the seventeenth century's beehive of scientific activity—about the importance of distinguishing between a musical ratio that is concordant and one that is pleasant or lovely.

These latter qualities, he explained, are impossible to measure: "What makes some people want to dance may make others want to cry. This is because it evokes ideas in our memory: for instance, those who have in the past enjoyed dancing to a certain tune feel a fresh wish to dance the moment they hear a similar one; on the other hand, if someone had never heard a galliard without some affliction befalling him, he would certainly grow sad when he heard it again. This is so certain that I reckon that if you whipped a dog five or six times to the sound of a violin, it would begin to howl and run away as soon as it heard that music again. . . ."

Hence, it is not possible to calculate which musical sounds are the most beautiful—we can only determine which are the most *perfect*. No wonder Descartes rejected equal temperament, a system that casually discards the simplest, purest musical ratios (such as 3:2 for the fifth or 4:3 for the fourth) for the sake of pleasing the ears. "As for the reasons given by your musicians who deny the [correct] proportions of the concords," he wrote to Mersenne with some exasperation, "I find them so absurd that I hardly know any more how to reply." With that, the most influential mind of his time shut the door on equal temperament.

Descartes's opinions molded much of his generation's thinking. Yet a scientific revolution was on the horizon—an era that would embrace the empirical above the ideological—and an alternate, post-Cartesian approach to nature (and to music) was in the making. (Descartes's reasoning was often stunning, but left unchecked it easily snagged on the nub of self-delusion. This was by no means an unusual problem. Mathematician John Napier gave the world logarithms in 1614—the marvelous mathematical device that enabled Kepler to compute planetary motion—after which the Scotsman used his invention to estimate the end of the world as occurring between 1688 and 1700.)

In 1611, poet John Donne wrote that philosophy had called everything into doubt, rendering the world "in pieces, all coherence gone." As the era progressed, however, Donne's fragments were being reassembled under the attentive ministrations of a new group known as the "virtuosos"—the name, explained chemist Robert Boyle, adopted by "those that understand and cultivate experimental philosophy." Among this assemblage were such luminaries of Western science as Boyle; Robert Hooke, the curator of experiments for England's Royal Society, and one of the first to argue that fossils proved the Book of Genesis wrong; Christiaan Huygens, the Dutch mathematician and astronomer who invented the pendulum clock and discovered the rings of Saturn; and, perhaps the greatest intellect of any age, Isaac Newton. Following Newton, Voltaire later recorded, few people still read Descartes, "whose works have in fact become totally useless. Newton also has very few readers," Voltaire declared, "because it requires great knowledge and sense to understand him. Everybody, however, talks about him."

After Newton, earlier philosophers of nature seemed, like the residents of Laputa in *Gulliver's Travels,* prisoners of a rigid, geometric fantasy. Jonathan Swift's caricatures—clumsy, awkward, and perplexed by every subject other than music and math—dined on mutton cut into equilateral triangles or sausages shaped like flutes, and spent long periods listening to the music of the spheres. Newton's universe was a

different sort of place: not merely mechanical but wondrously fluid, bristling with an electric and elastic spirit—a
calculus of continual change. His descriptions of things as
they *are* overwhelmed the old picture of what they logically
ought to be.

Along with changes in science came new perspectives in
other areas. Artists and musicians, growing increasingly concerned with the gravitational forces of the heart, searched
for hidden correspondences—bonds of sympathy—with
which to trigger emotional reactions in their audiences.

Several cultural trends had set the stage. There was, for
instance, the general moodiness that hung over the seventeenth-century psyche like a stale cloud. "You may as soon
separate weights from lead, heat from fire, moistness from
water, brightness from the sun, as misery, discontent, care,
calamity, danger, from a man," stated Robert Burton in his
1621 *Anatomy of Melancholy.*

At the same time, a fascination with the power of rhetoric—inherited from the Renaissance—continued. It was typi-
fied by George Puttenham's *Arte of English Poesie,* a 1589 book
in which the author announced the mission of creating "a
new and strange" rhetorical art able to "inveigle and appas-
sionate the mind." Henry Peacham's slightly earlier *Garden of
Eloquence* had already described an accomplished orator as
one able to draw from his hearers whatever *affection* he
desired: making them angry or pleased; causing them to
laugh, weep, love, or loathe. And this ability to move the
affections became a prime objective for artists. As we've seen,
early in the century, the Italian Gian Lorenzo Bernini thrilled
and terrified his audiences through dramatic presentations
filled with extraordinary special effects—the theatrical equiv-

alent of a roller-coaster ride. But even painters with more formal concerns, like Nicolas Poussin (about whom Bernini, striking his forehead, remarked, "He is a painter who works from there"), also became swept up in the movement. Poussin strove to find an equivalent in painting to the ancient musical modes—the scales through which the Greeks (the "inventors of all beautiful things," he wrote) were able to astonish their listeners.

Composers also cultivated these effects, and continued to stretch musical forms in new directions, making equal temperament—a system in which all tones and harmonies are usable regardless of where they may lie on the keyboard—more necessary than ever. Ironically, however, just as the new scientific landscape was taking shape, experimenters announced new acoustical evidence in support of . . . Descartes.

Their research centered on the behavior of vibrating strings. The philosopher had noted that when a string is plucked, other strings cut to lengths an octave or a fifth higher will sympathetically vibrate "of their own accord." He concluded that a single string contained within itself all those shorter strings with which it formed these harmonies. A decade later, Marin Mersenne, following Descartes's finding, reported that his ear could consistently detect *several* tones emanating simultaneously from a *single* string—an effect Isaac Beeckman chalked up to a string's inconsistent thickness. Descartes regarded a similar effect in bells as being due to their various parts vibrating at different speeds. These observations were now being scientifically corroborated and analyzed, and the explanations behind them turned out to be even more fascinating than previously imagined.

The Scientists Confer

In 1673, two Oxford men, William Noble and Thomas Pigot, discovered that once set in motion, a string divides itself into innumerable segments, each producing a discrete musical tone. The string acts, in effect, as if it were suspended over an invisible fretboard, on which unearthly fingers were choosing a secret melody. This mysterious phenomenon would profoundly influence music in the following century after further investigation by Joseph Sauveur, a mathematics teacher with a passionate interest in developing a "science of sound"—for which he would create the name *acoustics*. (Surprisingly, Sauveur—whose other activities included the calculation of chance in card games and the creation of waterworks at the castle of Chantilly—was, like Descartes, possessed of "neither voice nor ear" in music. He is often described, in fact, as having been deaf from birth. This is rather unlikely, though he did not speak before reaching the age of seven, and apparently had difficulty with oral communication throughout his life.)

Noble and Pigot's discovery confirmed that a single string tuned to a particular musical tone produces a whole *series* of soft, ancillary tones—sonic shadows that ring above every *do* or *re* or *mi* like unbidden harmonic ghosts. It seemed that nature had not only decreed the rules of musical harmony, but actually imbedded them in every vibrating object.

These *overtones* were just what Zarlino, Kepler, or Descartes would have predicted. They sound above the original note with tones corresponding to the octave (2:1), the fifth (3:2), and the major third (5:4). Thus, they whisper their support for those theorists who for centuries had declared these to be the purest, most natural, and most perfect harmonies of all.

Temperament

There had been hints of this phenomenon all along—for example, in Isaac Beeckman's rule for determining whether fifths were "justly tuned" (that is, vibrating in the ratio 3:2). You will know when they are exactly in the correct proportion, he explained, because then they will no longer produce the sound *wow wow.* The effect he was referring to, known as beating, occurs when two tones are *almost* equal in pitch, but not quite. The closer they are to a unison, the slower the "wow."

An explanation as to why imperfectly tuned *fifths*—which are not at all close in pitch—exhibit this behavior, however, had to await Noble and Pigot. It turned out that the clashes creating the *wow* actually occur between the *overtones* of these mistuned partners in harmony. (Imagine, for example, that the two tones being played were *do* and the *sol* an octave and a fifth higher. The second overtone produced by the string for *do* is that *sol.* If the two original tones are not in perfect concordance, then the *sol* produced as an overtone of *do* will not match the one being produced by the *sol* string. The slight mismatch between these two versions of *sol* will create *beating*—a rapid *wow wow wow* as they go in and out of phase with one another.)

All this was bad news for advocates of equal temperament. Without some form of temperament, no keyboard was adequate to the task of performing the most adventurous music of the period. Yet, the desirability of Descartes's "pure" harmonies was now bolstered by scientific evidence that they are indeed "natural." Equal temperament was being rejected as well by a growing group of musicians who appreciated the expressive possibilities inherent in *unequal* tunings such as mean-tone. The very inconsistencies in these tunings—the lack of uniformity in the sizes of their inter-vals—were seen by many as contributing to a more perfect musical grammar. In this view, hitting just the right pitch—not one that had been rounded off even by a fraction—was the equivalent of skillfully conjugating a verb or correctly declining a noun. Using equal temperament was like engaging in a coarser form of language, one that bypassed the subtle rules of syntax. Even if the resulting message can be understood, it will lack the eloquence and grace of a well-formed sentence.

Some attempted to solve the problem through mechanical innovation. Father Marin Mersenne, for example, urged the adoption of an instrument with nineteen keys, which would afford the player more opportunities to choose at any given moment the notes that would form perfect concords. "Although the nineteen keys of its octave may be, it seems, more difficult to play . . . ," he argued, "nevertheless the perfection of the harmony and the facility there is in tuning organs which use this . . . keyboard abundantly repays the difficulty of playing, which organists will be able to surmount in the space of one week or in very little time." Zarlino had a keyboard with nineteen notes to the octave constructed for him in 1548 by Maestro Domenico Pesarese; and Mersenne's design was the basis of a harpsichord built in Haarlem in 1639.

In truth, however, Mersenne might have been called as an expert witness by either side in the battle over equal temperament. Opponents could use his declaration that the lute—traditionally tuned in equal temperament—is the charlatan of instruments "because it passes off as good that which, on good instruments, is bad." Yet, Mersenne was also

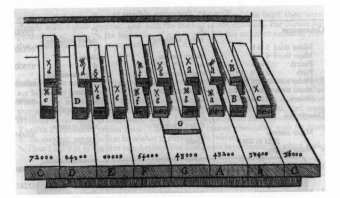

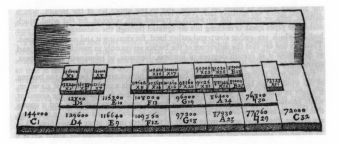

Keyboards designed with twenty-seven keys to the octave and thirty-two keys to the octave, from Marin Mersenne's *Harmonie universelle*

capable of offering a diplomatic compromise to the dispute, stating that "[although] those of us with a more delicate sense of hearing, such as the highly talented instrument maker Denis, can barely tolerate the temperament of equal [steps]...it satisfied other very experienced musicians." (Jean Denis, organist at Saint-Barthélemy in Paris and author of a 1643 treatise on harpsichord tuning, was adamantly against equal temperament. Then again, he seems to have been a rather intolerant fellow overall. In 1636 he was accused of having struck an apprentice and was forced to pay a fine to the boy's father.)

Proponents of equal temperament, on the other hand, could point to Mersenne's remarks in the third volume of his monumental *Harmonie universelle*. There, he clearly acknowledged the advantages of the approach: "Equal [steps] serve to avoid the embarrassment of [the] great multitude of intervals which arises from the discrepancies of the concords taken in their usual terms and ratios." With equal temperament, he stated, "composition will therefore be much easier and more agreeable, and a thousand things will be permitted that several [theorists] believe to be forbidden."

Mersenne often found himself at the difficult center of this dispute. Giovanni Battista Doni, Frescobaldi's ruthless foil—who accused the composer of both ignorance and moral degeneracy for supporting equal temperament—kept Mersenne well apprised of his progress in the fight against the new tuning. "An old man has been here," read one missive from Rome. This stranger, Doni explained, arrived, after living most of his life in Calabria and Sicily, with the idea of introducing a new invention—equal temperament on the harpsichord. "He found some among our musicians (ignorant as they are) who gave him credence," Doni continued. "But at last, recognizing the imperfection of this tuning, and [the fact that] good singers did not want to sing with such instruments (as I had predicted), they abandoned it, and everything is back to normal."

In all likelihood—despite bullying by the likes of Descartes and Doni—Mersenne probably agreed with the opinion of eighteenth-century theorist Johann Georg Neid-

D. Duflos's nineteenth-century etching of Marin Mersenne

hardt that "equal temperament brings with it its comfort and discomfort, like blessed matrimony." (Neidhardt seems to have had an unusually progressive attitude. He personally created more than two dozen different temperaments, believing that some were best suited for a village, others for a town, a city, or a royal court. The last was, in his opinion, the ideal setting for equal temperament.)

Another scientist keenly interested in the problem was Christiaan Huygens, the son of Dutch musician, poet, and statesman Constantijn Huygens. In addition to proposing the wave theory of light, inventing the pendulum clock, and discovering the rings of Saturn, Christiaan—who was proficient on the lute, flute, and harpsichord—used logarithms to calculate the division of the octave into thirty-one equal parts, which, he claimed, satisfactorily produced all the pitches anyone might need to play any piece.

His last work, published posthumously in Latin in 1698, was called *Cosmotheoros* (from the Greek *kosmos*, "universe," and *theoros*, "spectator"—and translated into English that year as *The Celestial Worlds Discover'd*). It has an unusual premise. After noting that one fully appreciates home only after being away, the author takes a flight of imagination to other planets, then returns to assess musical life on earth as it might be viewed by aliens. Since both the universe itself and music have a geometrical structure, wrote Huygens, music must exist on other planets. Believing that all people sing the same musical intervals, Huygens concluded that both the just-intonation musical scale (with pure thirds and fifths) and the need for temperament were universal—interplanetary—phenomena. His proposal to settle the predicament was, naturally, to construct keyboards with many extra keys.

One of his designs—an instrument capable of playing thirty-one tones in each octave—utilized two rows of keys: a bottom row with the normal twelve, an upper row with nineteen. He invented a movable keyboard that slid on a rail so that it could be repositioned along thirty-one strings, and thereby select the correct tones for any given piece. Models of these movable keyboards, designed to fit over ordinary harpsichords, were, he reported, actually constructed in Paris.

Temperament

Another extraordinary inventor of the time was a military engineer named Juan Caramuel y Lobkowitz, who served as an advisor to King Ferdinand III in Prague. By 1647, Lobkowitz had already used logarithms to develop a mathematical measure for accurate tuning. Moving to Prague in 1649, he continued to apply scientific techniques to music, producing a stunning assortment of keyboard instruments in the process. One employed wheels spinning against strings to produce a sustained sound—like the viola organista created by Leonardo da Vinci, but with small quills added along the circumference of each wheel. He designed an *upright* clavichord—a delicate, soft-sounding forerunner to the piano. It used a wooden mechanism for raising hammers to strike the strings, and lead weights to bring them down again. Clavichords normally sit on a tabletop, with their strings parallel to the ground. The vertical shape of Lobkowitz's version was a matter of necessity, he explained: He built it because of a lack of storage space to accommodate long, flat instruments.

Lobkowitz proposed equal temperament for the organ and the clavichord and built an instrument called the *organum panarchicum,* which placed a black key after every white one (as opposed to five blacks to every seven whites as on today's keyboards). He based the idea, he said, on an ancient Greek instrument that allowed any key to serve as *do.* Because of the perfect symmetry of its keyboard design, the organum panarchicum would allow musicians to use the same fingerings no matter where their hands were placed. (To help orient the player, the black notes were made a little fatter, and the white keys above them were projected out a bit by means of nails.)

His *abacus enneacordos,* on the other hand, had only two

black keys in each octave (while the white ones were distinguished from one another by an alternation of ivory and wood). Some of these conceptions lived on for some time: C.P.E. Bach reported that his father, Johann Sebastian, had seen organs with no black keys at all; and as late as the nineteenth century, classical pianist and composer Muzio Clementi came across pianos with only two in each octave.

Lobkowitz also designed the *automatum panharmonicum,* an organ that operated like a modern player piano, using wooden rolls into which canals had been cut. And for those who refused to go along with his advocacy of equal temperament he designed a harpsichord with extra (split) keys.

It's not surprising that a flurry of activity around the mechanics of musicmaking should arise at so many different places at the same time. Science was developing rapidly, due in part to the unprecedented free flow of information between researchers. Rome's Accademia dei Lincei (the Academy of the Lynx-eyed, which Galileo joined in 1611), organized after a similar organization founded in Naples, had given rise to societies in Florence, England, France, and elsewhere. Each group organized conclaves and issued journals—such as the *Philosophical Transactions* of England's Royal Society, and the *Journal des savants* of the French Académie des Sciences—to propagate the latest findings and contentions of leading experimentalists.

After 1650, though, the front line in the scientific revolution was just as often located in a different sort of meeting place, called the coffeehouse.

The dark elixir known as coffee was once considered so dangerous it was banned in Mecca in 1511. But six years later it was all the rage in Istanbul; and by 1615 it had conquered

Venice. An anonymous treatise in Lyon in 1671 outlined its winning properties: Coffee, it claimed, "dries up all cold and damp humours, drives away wind, strengthens the liver, relieves dropsies by its purifying quality . . . extraordinary relief after over-eating or over-drinking. Nothing better for those who eat a lot of fruit." Once introduced to European society, it became an irresistible lubricant to intellectual conversation and social interplay. When the Sicilian Francesco Procopio Coltelli set up his café, Le Procope, in Paris's rue des Fosses–Saint-Germain in 1686, the greatest minds of the age—Voltaire, Diderot, d'Alembert, and Rousseau—regularly met there to drink the bitter blend and debate the issues of the day.

Clientele frequenting these new enterprises found another exotic refreshment equally alluring: chocolate, which came from Mexico by way of Spain. In the 1650s, Cardinal Richelieu learned of it from Spanish nuns who had brought it to France; his servants reported that he took it regularly to moderate the vapors of his spleen. Yet this substance was no mere tonic, as one Gemelli Careri learned in 1693 when he offered some to a Turkish Aga. The Aga, Careri recalled, "was either intoxicated by it or smoke from the tobacco produced that effect, for he flared up at me violently, saying that I had made him drink a liquor to upset him and take away his powers of judgment." Perhaps it was those very qualities that made the drink so attractive to Newton's chief scientific rival, the impetuous Robert Hooke, who garnered a reputation for imbibing huge quantities of the sweet delicacy.

Hooke, the son of a minister who "died by suspending himself," was curator of experiments for England's Royal

Society and author of *Micrographia,* the first work to reveal the world as seen through the eyepiece of a microscope. The inventor of the escapement mechanism used in clocks, and one of the first to introduce tension springs in watches (an idea that embroiled him in a dispute over first authorship with Huygens), Hooke was the ascetic Newton's opposite in every way—a voluptuary and carouser who held court in the coffeehouses and taverns so often, and with such verve, that he found himself caricatured in a popular farce called *The Virtuoso.* (After attending a performance of the play in June 1676, he was convulsed with humiliation. "Damned Doggs," he noted in his diary. "Cindica me Deus [God avenge me]. People almost pointed.") But Hooke's rowdy sociability made for easy collaborations with others. And the results— in physics, optics, and biology—were staggeringly abundant. In Hooke's case, the incentives were manifold: As the *Journal des savants* quipped, science and math now achieved such popular acclaim that many women made the squaring of the circle a requirement of anyone with amorous intentions.

Like Mersenne, Huygens, and Newton, Hooke was deeply interested in the connections between the physical and musical worlds. He used his microscope to investigate the fabric of a butterfly's wings before determining the speed of a fly's by establishing the musical note it produced while in flight. But his interests went deeper. Indeed, anticipating a branch of physics that would come to prominence three hundred years later as "string theory," he described the universe as being made up of invisible, vibrating particles: "like so many equal musical strings" working in harmony. And in an essay entitled "A Curious Dissertation," posthumously published in the *Philosophical Transactions,* Hooke discussed some of the mysterious effects ascribed to music through the ages.

Music as an art was "exercised by the infancy of the world, being used almost as soon, if not before language, so we find it the first thing that pleases and delights," he wrote. Though recognizing, along with Descartes, that the same sounds can bring about different emotional reactions—bells rung for a funeral provoke grief, while those for a wedding add to mirth—Hooke believed that music's potency was indisputable. It had the ability, he insisted, to neutralize the venom of a tarantula: a result "so well known in Italy . . . that there are few question it." (His source for this was probably Zarlino.) Furthermore, he studiously reported, in Denmark, a musician playing the wrong scale threw the king into a violent frenzy, "wherein he not only fell upon his dear friends and counselors, beating and kicking them, but went on to kill several of them," until the musician altered his tune "and playing in a more soft, mild and effeminate strain, reduced him to himself again." (Much of our own contemporary music seems designed to produce the same agitated effect on audiences; but, luckily, most of it falls short of this mark.)

Finding science and myth so easily coexistent in the work of a renowned scientist reflects the perspective of Hooke's time. The model was set a century before him by another scientist, John Dee—a Merlin-like character with long white beard and magician's robe who was charged with attempted murder against Queen Mary Tudor by means of sorcery and ended up becoming her personal astrologer. Unlike Hooke, however, Dee's pursuits in mathematics and science were overshadowed by his reputation in astrology (an art that served him well until the day the heavens informed him it was time to exchange wives with one of his students).

Clearly, even at the end of the seventeenth century, the line between science and magic remained paper thin. When German alchemist Hennig Brand conjured up a chemical that glowed in the dark and presented it to Charles II, revealing only that it somehow belonged to "the body of man," the king was truly astounded and grateful (until Robert Boyle figured out how to obtain phosphorus from human urine). As late as 1692, Jacques Aymer was heralded in France for his ability to detect criminals by means of a hazel twig that twitched in his hands. No less a scientific figure than England's royal astronomer John Flamsteed traveled great distances to be stroked by the charlatan Valentine Greatrakes, who claimed to cure scrofula (a condition characterized by glandular swellings in the neck and respiratory problems). Over the years, King Charles II touched as many as a hundred thousand scrofula sufferers who lined up to receive *his* healing; when he tried to put an end to the routine by telling one, "God give you better health and more sense," he was angrily denounced. (It's hardly shocking that so many were afflicted with this malady. London in 1661, with its refuse-filled Thames and belching smokestacks, was described in a report requested by the king as resembling more "the suburbs of hell, than an assembly of rational creatures. . . . The weary traveler, at many miles' distance, sooner smells than sees the city. . . .")

Indeed, the greatest scientist of all, Newton, remained preoccupied with alchemy his entire life. He once joked that the early onset of his silver hair was a result of too much contact with the alchemist's tool, mercury. On a less humorous note, the liquid metal might actually have been responsible for Newton's nervous breakdown, which culminated in a paranoid frenzy during which he lashed out at friends. In a particularly painful letter, he accused the philosopher John Locke—whose *Essay Concerning Human Understanding* in 1687 delivered a decisive blow to those who clung to a belief in innate ideas over sensory experience—of seeking his destruction by attempting to "embroil me with women." Despite the compelling drama of those high-flown mystical stories conveyed by Hooke, however, for Newton the grand puzzle of the universe was a matter for experiment and observation, not anecdote.

On the other hand, Newton sometimes found confirmation of his own theories in questionable sources—detecting in the Pythagoras legend, for example, a cloaked announcement of the laws of gravity. According to later tradition, the ancient philosopher of Croton was said to have capped his discovery of musical proportion with another, more complicated finding—the rules governing the effect of tension on a vibrating string. Though Galilei is now credited with the finding, Newton believed that Pythagoras knew that when varying the *weights* attached to the ends of the strings rather than string length, the proportions had to be squared and inverted. To Newton, the Pythagoras story was a parable; its true intent was to reveal "that the weights of the planets towards the sun were reciprocally as the squares of their distances from the sun."

A desire to find a connection with the Greek sage was understandable. Many of Pythagoras's mathematical experi-

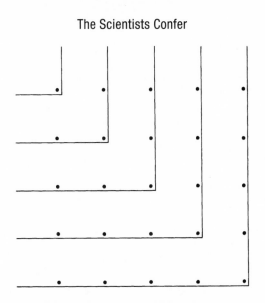

Pythagoras used geometric figures to represent mathematical progressions. His series of odd numbers drawn in the form of larger and larger squares is actually a simple way of seeing the differences between "squared numbers": $(2 \times 2) - (1 \times 1) = 3$; $(3 \times 3) - (2 \times 2) = 5$; $(4 \times 4) - (3 \times 3) = 7$, and so on.

ments did produce results uncannily similar to physical law. For example, Galileo discovered that the distances traversed by a falling object during equal intervals of time follow the odd-number series: measured in quarter-seconds, an object will fall first one foot, then three, then five. By the eighth second the number of feet fallen will be sixty-four—and this replicates the results of the progression Pythagoras created through his series of "square numbers": $1 + 3 + 5 + 7 + 9 + 11 + 13 + 15 = 8^2$.

In addition, Newton's quest, like Pythagoras's, was a spiritual one. Surely it would have been difficult to overlook the resonance between the images of Pythagoras at the blacksmith's furnace and the alchemist at his own. Newton even adopted the pseudonym Jeova Sanctus Unus—an anagram of the Latinized Isaacus Neuutonus—linking his own name with the declaration that Jehovah is the one holy God. For Newton, who wrote in 1675 that "perhaps the whole frame of nature may be nothing but various contextures of some certain ethereal spirits," music, light, and the planets were simply different constituents of one eternal, divine harmony. Why shouldn't the laws of gravity be the same as the laws governing musical strings?

Because of this, Newton studied tunings and temperaments the way Hooke studied the butterfly. He found musical proportions in the distances between the bands of colors that are produced by light projected through a prism. Like Lobkowitz, he created a standard unit of measure for determining the sizes of musical intervals, and calculated the precise values of pitches found in various scales. And he proposed tuning schemes of his own.

Of course, by this time, almost everyone was getting into the act. Even the famous diarist Samuel Pepys vowed to develop a "theory of music not yet ever made in the world." According to his diary entries, Pepys set out to find a book by "Marsanne, in French," and, failing to find it, bought a copy of Descartes's treatise on music, then attended a lecture by Hooke and William Brouncker, the first president of the Royal Society, on music's concords and discords. Unsatisfied with any of the explanations offered of why some harmonies work and others don't, he reiterated in his diary a determination to find better answers himself—after which, however, we hear from Pepys no further mention of the subject.

Hooke's lecturing partner, Lord Brouncker, who was chancellor to Queen Catherine and keeper of her Great Seal, published an English translation of Descartes's *Compendium* in 1653 and was also one of the first to use logarithms in musical calculations. He (of course) devised his own temperament system based on an aesthetic proportion favored by the ancient Greeks known as the Golden Section; the ratio that creates it can be found throughout the natural world, governing, for example, the shapes of sunflowers and of nautilus shells. Unfortunately, Brouncker's tuning turned out to be absolutely unusable in the performance of music—a fact he explained away by saying that the human sense of hearing is not really so perfect that the faults in his system much mattered. Somehow, his reputation as a music theorist remained intact nevertheless.

Some scholars assert that Newton's interest was, like Brouncker's, not actually in music at all, but only in the mathematical problems associated with it. The assessment is based in part on a casual remark Newton made at the end of his life bemoaning a night at the opera. However, at the beginning of the eighteenth century, carping about opera was a favorite intellectual pastime, practiced by such figures as Johnson, Swift, Addison, and Steele. (Addison once declared that in opera the fundamental rule is that "nothing is capable of being well set to music that is not nonsense.") Despite his negative remarks, in his unpublished treatise, Newton seems sincerely concerned with improving the state of musical practice. He even hand-copied a manual on how to play the viol, presumably to help him evaluate the practical applications of his proposals.

Nevertheless, his solution to the temperament problem was, in the end, unremarkable. Equal temperament, he asserted, "only assists towards continuing the imperfections of music: And 'tis unworthy of philosophers to contrive the corrupting of the true proportions." Newton's remedy boiled down to the cumbersome method of offering performers a greater-than-usual choice of notes to play. In the end, Newton remained convinced that the simple ratios governing musical concords had indeed been consecrated by nature.

Soon, however, other scientists would put that idea finally to rest. Five years after the publication of Robert Hooke's *A Curious Dissertation* on the power of music, the mathematician, doctor, and physicist Daniel Bernoulli (a name still recognized among young science students for his basic laws of fluid mechanics) discovered that the series of overtones resonating above a string's fundamental musical tone extends much farther than anyone had suspected. A close inspection revealed that the sounds of the octave, the fifth, and the third ringing above that initial note are only the beginning: They are joined by a multitude of higher tones, difficult to hear because of their diminishing strength. These additional sounds expand the series endlessly with tones that are not generally harmonious. Most, in fact, create peculiar, dissonant harmonies that were long considered *unnatural*. Bernoulli found that the individual character of an instrument's sound—that which gives it its own special personality—is determined largely by which of these myriad overtones are enhanced, and which are suppressed.

Thus, all vibrating bodies naturally float in an ocean of discord. What science had previously supported, it now exposed as fiction. The idea that the justly tuned concordances—harmonies produced by the simple ratios of 2:1, 3:2, 4:3, and 5:4—are preferred by nature had, it seemed, been permanently destroyed.

13

Liberty, Equality, Adversity

Stretch or contract me, thy poore debter,
This is but tuning of my breast,
To make the musick better.

—George Herbert, "The Temper"

As England's scientific revolution rippled across the Channel to France, its message of systematic doubt inspired a fresh wave of thinkers itching for change. Philosophers like Voltaire, Denis Diderot, and Jean Le Rond d'Alembert—the latter two co-editors of the Enlightenment's centerpiece, the great *Encyclopedia*—marveled at the way the English had so easily cast off old habits of mind. Now it was their turn.

Voltaire visited the island across the Channel and, heady with its freethinking atmosphere, wrote twenty-four enthusiastic *Letters Concerning the English Nation* (published in London in 1733). Back in France, the book was officially denounced as "scandalous, contrary to religion, good morals and the respect due to authority," and ordered burned by the public hangman in the courtyard of the Palais de Justice. Poet Heinrich Heine later commented sarcastically that there had been no need to ban Voltaire's letters—they would have been influential even without the state's negative sanction. Nevertheless, the reaction certainly gave his cause a boost.

And what subversive ideas they contained! The English, having turned toward experience rather than otherworldly mythology as the basis of truth, declared Voltaire, had learned to tolerate different faiths and to resist the power of kings—thus protecting their own natural rights. These themes became a rallying cry for the intelligentsia; little did anyone realize where it would all end—on the sharp edge of a guillotine.

The French "Age of Reason" threw into question every element of the social contract; its partisans relentlessly skewered religion, art, politics, and even marriage. "I think of the existence of God, in relation to a nation, as I do of marriage," wrote Diderot, who appears to have taken full advantage of the fact that his physical charms matched his intellectual gifts. "The latter as an institution, the former as a notion, are excellent for three or four persons of sound intellect, but fatal to the common run of men. The vow of indissoluble marriage makes, and is bound to make, almost as many wretches as there are married people. The belief in God makes, and is bound to make, almost as many fanatics as there are believers."

Of course, it was no news that marriage might be practiced as a social convenience rather than a bond of the heart. Montesquieu made the traveler in his *Persian Letters* report that in Paris, "a husband who would wish to have sole possession of his wife would be regarded as a disturber of public happiness." And the phenomenon was by no means restricted to Parisians. In a 1716 letter from Vienna, Lady Mary Montagu asserted, "'Tis the established custom for every lady to have two husbands, one that bears the name, and another that performs the duties. And these engagements are so well known that it would be a downright affront, and publicly resented, if you invited a woman of quality to dinner without at the same time inviting her two attendants. . . ."

Indeed, in the battle of the sexes, the resourcefulness of women was not to be underestimated. When Claudine Alexandrine de Tencin accepted administrative responsibility for Charles Joseph de La Fresnai's fortune and then refused to give it back, he killed himself in her rooms in 1726, and she was sent to the Bastille briefly. But within two years her Tuesday-evening salons were being attended by the city's intellectual elite, including Fontenelle, Montesquieu, and Marivaux. (Ten years later, a rival salon held by Madame Du Deffand drew Voltaire, Diderot, and d'Alembert.)

Attacking religion was riskier business than attacking marriage, but the church's critics, emboldened by the atmosphere of intellectual freedom, could be wildly daring. Jean Meslier, a priest whose radical *Testament* was published by Voltaire in a somewhat softened form, declared flatly: "I will not sacrifice my reason . . . I will not give up experience . . . I will not distrust my senses." A close reading of biblical evidence, he asserted, clearly showed God to be "infinitely more wicked than the most wicked of men."

Diderot's *Letter on the Blind, for the Use of Those Who See*, a fictitious account of the life of blind mathematician Nicholas

Saunderson, went a step further by making even atheism reasonable. "If you wish me to believe in God," he had Saunderson proclaim, "you must make me touch him." Diderot was arrested for his efforts and, in Voltaire's phrase, "provided by the king with free lodgings" for a short time. Nevertheless, rational speculation, having led to the unthinkable, was now virtually free of all limitations. The Scottish philosopher David Hume, while attending a gathering at Baron Paul Heinrich Dietrich von Holbach's, told his host that he doubted the actual existence of atheists. Holbach, whose home served as a sort of "Café d'Europe" for the rich and famous of his day, quickly assured him, "Here you are at table with seventeen."

It couldn't all be blamed on the English. Fervor was as natural to Parisians as the state of dampened spirits known as "spleen" was to their more restrained colleagues across the Channel. Diderot once raised the question of the dour English character with a Scottish guest: "My head is never free," reported the visitor. "It is so heavy at times that it feels weight which drags me forward, and would carry me out of a window into the street, or headlong to the bottom of a river if I stood on the bank. I have gloomy ideas. I am sad and bored; I feel uncomfortable everywhere, I wish for nothing." The French, on the other hand, wished for everything—passionately. What's more, they had no doubt of their ability to have it. "Our century believes itself destined to change the laws in every kind," wrote d'Alembert.

For a while, it actually seemed possible. Art, philosophy, and literature were flourishing. A project to translate Ephraim Chambers's two-volume *Cyclopoedia, or a Universal Dictionary of Arts and Sciences,* published in London in 1728, grew into something bigger and better: the creation of an unprecedented, immense French encyclopedia under the editorship of Diderot and d'Alembert. Even the rule of entire kingdoms seemed to be within the philosophers' reach. Voltaire succeeded for a time in cultivating Prussia's Frederick the Great from a mere royal into a philosopher king. After watching the death of his father (a man who, in a tyrannical rage, had once tried to do away with his son and heir by beating him, dragging him to a window, and tying the curtain cord around his throat), Frederick announced to Voltaire: "I have witnessed the last moments of a king, his agony, his death. On coming to the throne I had no need of that lesson to be disgusted with the vanity of human grandeur. . . ." The new ruler praised the English constitution as a model of good government, ordered the public granaries opened to the poor, and abolished the use of torture in criminal trials.

As time went on, however, he predictably became more king and less philosopher, and his personal relationship with Voltaire, after undergoing severe trials, ended in disenchantment. The blame, however, was probably not all Frederick's. Poet and scientist Albrecht von Haller was undoubtedly right when he informed Casanova that "Monsieur de Voltaire is a man who deserves to be known, although, contrary to the laws of physics, many people have found him greater at a distance."

Concerns about the well-being of the masses produced strides in the betterment of public health as well. Voltaire, for one, championed the use of condoms (advocated by Fallopio in 1564) to prevent venereal disease. As Lord Chesterfield cautioned his son about syphilis: "In love a man may lose his

heart with dignity . . . if he loses his nose he loses his character in the bargain." Nevertheless, quacks persisted. The best
known was Franz Anton Mesmer. Parisians flocked to him en
masse to be "mesmerized" by his alleged magnetic waves;
Louis XVI even offered to establish a Magnetic Institute
under his directorship. However, the Académie des Sciences
set up a committee of scientists, including Benjamin Franklin, to investigate Mesmer's claims. Their report was not
favorable; in the end the French Revolution declared him an
imposter and confiscated his considerable fortune.

Despite these small setbacks, it was the dawn of a new
day and a new world. Yet, there was no unanimity among the
philosophers about exactly how that world should be shaped.
Jean-Jacques Rousseau, who arrived in Paris with the inten-
tion of promoting a new system of musical notation (a project he swiftly abandoned after composer Jean-Philippe
Rameau dismissed it as impractical), began his philosophical
career with a prizewinning essay in which he charged that
the glorious revival of arts and sciences was actually a corrupting influence on public morals. Egypt, Greece, and
Rome all fell as a result of luxury and intellectual pride, he
asserted. Could France be far behind?

This was the first airing of a view for which Rousseau
would later become famous: that man in his natural state is
good—it is society that perverts him. For Rousseau, pre-
societal man was, to take an image from his essay "On the
Origin of Inequality," like the earth in its original fertile
splendor—robust and whole, with boundless forests not yet
mutilated by the axe. The opening of his novel *Émile, or Concerning Education,* puts it succinctly: "Everything is good in
leaving the hands of the creator of things; everything de-

generates in the hands of man." Government, claimed Rousseau, is evil, imposed by rich schemers; marriage is ruinous; private property breeds greed and war; the proper model of a decent life resides in the innocent primitive. Edmund Burke was sufficiently alarmed at Rousseau's ideas about relations between men and women to accuse his followers of turning gallant love—"that fine flower of youthfulness and gentility"—into an "indelicate, sour, gloomy, ferocious medley of pedantry and lewdness. . . ."

The noble savage had already fascinated many eighteenth-century writers, including Lord Shaftesbury and Daniel Defoe, whose story of Robinson Crusoe and his man Friday struck Rousseau as the best book available on the natural sciences. It was the talk of intellectual circles when a Swedish missionary, delivering a sermon to a tribe of American Indians in 1700, was challenged by their chief, who asked, among other questions, why, if Christians have superior knowledge of God, their morals are so depraved. This famous incident spurred Benjamin Franklin to write his *Remarks Concerning the Savages of North America* in 1784, in which the tribal spokesman states, "What you have told us . . . is all very good. It is indeed bad to eat apples. It is better to make them all into cider."

Rousseau's theories about music—man's most powerful medium for conveying thoughts and feelings—were colored by these notions. Melody, like language, said Rousseau, was born of an erotic fervor: man's untamed impulses craving release. Springing from the deepest well of hunger, desire, pleasure, and sorrow, original melody "imitates the accents of language . . . [but it] has a hundred times more energy than speech itself." Unfortunately, believed Rousseau, along came civilization. As language was perfected, and melody subjected to rules, both lost their primitive powers. Music's raw poetic intensity became stifled through the imposition of artificial conventions.

Rousseau's assertions led to one of the most heated clashes in music history, his bitter dispute with the greatest French musician of the day, Rameau. From the beginning, no love was lost between them. Their first encounter involved Rameau's rejection of Rousseau's music notation system. The real hostility began in 1745, however, at a performance of Rousseau's attempt at an opera-ballet, *Les Muses galantes.* The work was unveiled at the home of an influential music patron named La Poplinière. Rousseau had asked Rameau to help with the writing of the score. When the composer begged off the assignment, Rousseau enlisted the aid of renowned musician and chess master François André Philidor instead.

Rameau accepted the invitation to hear the completed work with some reluctance, and in retrospect, it would have been better had he stayed home. "From the opening bars," remembered Rousseau, "Rameau began to let people understand by his outrageous praises that the music could not be mine. No part was performed without signs of impatience from him. . . . He accosted me with a brutality that scandalized everybody, maintaining that a section he had just heard was that of a consummate artist, and the rest that of an ignorant person who did not even know anything about music. . . ." Rousseau later admitted that the work was uneven. However, Rameau had thoroughly humiliated him, making it clear that the parts fixed up by Philidor were the only good ones. Rousseau longed for a chance to redeem his pride. The stage was set for a grand battle.

The loudest volley was a provocative *Lettre sur la musique française,* with which Rousseau launched what became known as "the War of the Buffoons," an extended argument pitting Italian opera against French (he scored additional points in his music articles for Diderot and d'Alembert's encyclopedia). The operas of Rameau, and of his predecessor Lully, Rousseau charged, were inferior to those of the Italians, in part simply by dint of the fact that they were sung in French. French was universally employed as the language of social discourse, just as Latin was the language of intellectual pursuit. (Indeed, it was reported that even Frederick the Great of Prussia refused to speak German—except to his horses, and even then only when they were secluded in their stables.) As a language devoted to reason, French was capable only of producing reasonable things—thus it was inherently unmusical. The dulcet, liquid tones of Italian were far better suited to the expression of passion.

Even more important, however, was the fact that Italian composers focused on "natural" melody rather than on "artificial" harmony, the latter being the chief concern of the French. For Rousseau, all music and all language sprang from that first melodic utterance of human emotion, an unrestrained cry emanating from the human breast. The French, with their emphasis on harmony, had cultivated a tradition far removed from those simple, natural beginnings.

"Nature does nothing that is not correct," Diderot declared in *Notes on Painting.* "Every form, whether beautiful or ugly, has its cause, and of all extant beings there isn't a single one that's not just as it should be." In an era of uncertain rules, nature stood as the great arbiter of truth, not only in science, but in art as well. It was no surprise that Rousseau rested his claim squarely on her authority.

But so did Rameau. A musician whose art is formed solely "by comparisons that are within reach of his sensations, can at best only excel in certain directions," the composer warned. "Moreover, as he draws on his imagination for everything without any help from art in its relation to expression, he ends by exhausting himself. . . . What one should seek therefore, for the theater, is a musician who has studied nature before painting her and who by his knowledge has been able to choose colors and shades the relation of which with the required expressions is borne in upon him by his judgment and taste." Who, then, was closer to nature: the untamed primitive or the practiced observer?

Diderot underwent a change of opinion on this subject over time. His earliest idea of creative genius was of a mind filled with an elemental fire: impulsive, unbridled, and oblivious of itself—Rousseau's primal man. But after meeting the English actor David Garrick, who demonstrated his brilliant ability to convey any emotion at the drop of a hat, Diderot reversed course, describing the true artist as self-possessed and deliberate—a master of his resources. To capture nature requires a command of detail, and it's not an easy task: "Imagine . . . the canvas's depth of field subdivided, in whatever direction, by an infinite number of infinitely tiny spatial planes," he wrote, describing the intricacies of portraying brightness and shade naturally in painting:

> The difficult problem is the proper disposition of light
> and shadow, within each of these planes as well as on

each infinitely thin slice of the objects occupying them; these are visual echoes, the intermingled reflections of all this light. When this effect is produced (but where and how is this accomplished?) the eye is transfixed; it remains stationary. Satisfied everywhere, it is everywhere refreshed; it moves forward, it moves backward, it retraces its course. Everything is connected, everything coheres. Art and artist are forgotten. It's no longer a question of a canvas but of nature, of a portion of the universe.

For Rameau a detailed study of nature revealed that harmony, rather than language or melody, served as the real root of musical expression. Harmony itself, he claimed, is governed by a universal natural phenomenon known as the *sonorous body:* the tendency of a vibrating object to radiate not only a fundamental tone, but higher overtones corresponding to the octave, the fifth, and the third. This phenomenon had by now gotten significant scientific play. In fact, even before Descartes raised the issue, it had appeared in Aristotle's writings on physics. The ancient writer had suggested that a low musical tone contains the tone an octave above it, and noted that when a high string on a lyre is stopped from vibrating the string an octave below can be heard to resonate. Now Rameau revamped the behavior of a sonorous body into an archetype from which the rules of music should be derived. Nature loved harmony, he asserted, and the progressions and juxtapositions of her sounds—their pushing and pulling toward and away from each other—served as the basis for music's expressive possibilities.

The argument between Rousseau and Rameau held profound implications for the fight over musical temperament. If music depended on harmony for its expressiveness, then equal temperament (by midcentury it would come to be called "Rameau's tuning") was crucial, because it offered any keyboard instrument a unique ability to facilitate harmonic movement.

As the seventeenth century gave way to the eighteenth, things seemed to be moving in Rameau's direction.

The era opened with a new musical rage captivating the royal courts: Pantaleon Hebenstreit and his amazing giant hammered dulcimers. An itinerant musician and onetime dancing master, Hebenstreit's career had been going nowhere until he hit on the idea of building his nine-foot instruments with two hundred strings stretched over two soundboards, and of mastering a virtuoso technique for playing them with two sticks. The effect had audiences spellbound. Some swore he could convey a different feeling with every note. Louis XIV was so moved, he suggested renaming the dulcimer the "pantaleon." When Hebenstreit ended a long, contented life in 1750 at the court of Dresden, his salary was almost double that of Johann Sebastian Bach. His fame was so great that the early parlor piano became known as a "pantalon."

There were connections between Hebenstreit's enormous dulcimer and the emergence of the piano, that other keyboard instrument that produced a similarly warm sound—and dynamic flexibility—by propelling hammers against strings. One link was German organ builder Gottfried Silbermann.

Silbermann had been responsible for manufacturing Hebenstreit's instruments before 1727; then the two had a falling out. Neither man had a gift for diplomacy. Hebenstreit was, after all, a star. Silbermann, who reputedly took an axe to instruments he found substandard, tended to be intolerant even of small annoyances; he once smashed the windows of a church while trying to find the source of a rattle. As the argument between them grew heated, Hebenstreit was granted a royal order forbidding Silbermann to build any more "pantaleons"; so the instrument maker turned his skills to the manufacture of pianos. (Another German who claimed to be the piano's "inventor," Christoph Gottlieb Schröter, also cited Pantaleon Hebenstreit as the inspiration for *his* version of the instrument.)

For many musicians, the invention of the piano was a wish come true. Composer and keyboardist François Couperin had pleaded in print for the creation of just such an instrument in 1711. He would be "forever grateful," wrote Couperin, to anyone who could render the monotonous harpsichord capable of expression. Despite its many favorable points—Couperin conceded it was "perfect as to its compass, and brilliant in itself"—the harpsichord's mechanism, based on the plucking of strings, left the instrument irreversibly stuck on one dynamic level, unable to render its individual tones softer (*piano*) or louder (*forte*) at any given moment. Couperin's fellow Frenchman the lawyer and inventor Jean Marius answered the composer's call with his own version of the piano in 1716. All seemed unaware that Bartolomeo Cristofori, a curator of instruments for the Medicis, had already produced a keyboard capable of soft or loud sounds depending on the strength used to strike its keys (hence the name *pianoforte,* or "soft-loud," today shortened simply to *piano*) by 1700. And even he wasn't the first.

Christoph Gottlieb Schröter by Styfang

There was, for example, the pianolike *dulce melos,* diagrammed by Henricus Arnaut of Zwolle—a physician, astronomer, and musician in the Burgundian court of Philip the Good—apparently in use as early as 1440. And several sixteenth-century Italian documents make mention of keyboards capable of dynamic gradation. But Cristofori's invention was innovative and marvelous—a subtle, complex machine with a spring-assisted system to allow the hammers

Cristofori's piano, 1711

to rebound immediately after striking their targeted strings. (Silbermann's pianos, which came a bit later, were modeled after Cristofori's.) By 1732, music was already being published for the new invention—a set of pieces by Ludovico Giustini, written for what the composer referred to as the "Keyboard of Soft and Loud Commonly Called the Little Hammers."

Of course, the early piano had its critics as well. Composer Christian Friedrich Daniel Schubart called the pantalon piano a tinny "dwarf" incapable of nuance and predicted it wouldn't last. He found the older, soft-voiced clavichord "tender and responsive to your soul's every inspiration, and it

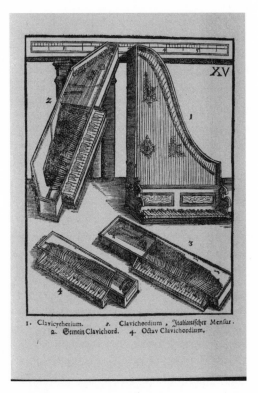

Clavichords and clavicytherium from Michael Praetorius's *Musica getutscht* (Basel, 1511)

is here that you will find your heart's soundboard. . . . Sweet melancholy, languishing love, parting grief, the soul's communing with God, uneasy forebodings, glimpses of Paradise through suddenly rent clouds, sweetly purling tears . . . in the contact with those wonderful strings and caressing keys." (Poor Schubart, imprisoned by Duke Carl Eugen of Württemberg for insulting his mistress, was forced for ten years to write music from behind the confining walls of the fortress Hohenasperg. Who can imagine what the clavichord must have meant to him during that period?)

Perhaps the greatest composer in history, Johann Sebastian Bach, had a mixed reaction to Silbermann's first pianos. He liked the tone (except for some weakness in the upper portion of the instrument), but found the movement of the keys too sluggish. True to form, Silbermann fumed over the criticism. Over time, though, he wisely decided to heed Bach's advice. Silbermann improved his instruments to the point that Bach not only played and enjoyed them (at the court of Frederick the Great and apparently also at a concert Bach himself organized in Leipzig), but even sold one, acting as Silbermann's agent, to Count Branitzky of Bialystok.

In addition to the expressive range it offered performers through dynamic shading, the piano also produced a full-bodied, sonorous tone, in stark contrast to the biting clangor of the harpsichord. Indeed, its timbre, like the lute's, made the modified musical intervals of equal-tempered tuning easy to take; and pieces that especially benefited by this feature now proliferated. The piano's popularity grew by leaps and bounds.

Among the composers advancing the musical frontiers toward the adoption of the new equal-tempered tuning was Johann Caspar Ferdinand Fischer. His keyboard work *Ariadne musica* of 1715 was based on the ancient myth of Ariadne, in which the heroine saves her lover, Theseus, from a labyrinth by secretly marking his path to safety with a red thread. In Fischer's *Ariadne,* the music threads its way through twenty different major and minor "keys"—each piece in the collection revolves around a different central tone (a "tonal center" or "key center") like a sun with its own particular constellation of planets. The planets in one key—the scale tones that work perfectly with a particular tonal center—would not necessarily be in tune with those of another when mean-tone tunings were used. Composer Johann Pachelbel had already included music in seventeen different keys (each one revolving around a different tone) in his keyboard suites of 1683, and in 1719 Johann Mattheson offered an organ work that used twenty-four possible tonal centers—two (one in major and one in minor) for each of the twelve tones. Johann Sebastian Bach based his monumental *Well-Tempered Clavier* (which also used all twenty-four major and minor keys) on Fischer's *Ariadne*—he even borrowed some of Fischer's themes for the piece.

Such wide-ranging works were a direct challenge to mean-tone temperament, since no keyboard can execute all these different scales in mean-tone tuning without falling prey to the "wolves." Writing on behalf of Johann Sebastian Bach, Georg Andreas Sorge castigated Silbermann, who adhered to mean-tone temperament, for using a "barbaric" tuning. And a tradition holds that Bach told Silbermann, "You *tune* the organ in the manner you please, and I *play* the organ in the key I please," and emphasized his point by performing music in a key guaranteed to send the instrument maker fleeing to escape the ensuing racket.

At around this time an important new musical form was also emerging. The *sonata*—a structure that continues to occupy composers even to this day—evolved especially in the works of composer and keyboard artist Domenico Scarlatti. (Though Scarlatti was Italian, the hundreds of keyboard works for which he is best known were composed at the

Spanish court—which had on hand several pianos—while he was in the service of his student the princess Maria Barbara.)

The term "sonata" was first used merely to describe a piece divided into two distinct, repeated sections. But slowly it came to signify something more complex: a vehicle in which a musical theme was not merely stated and repeated, but transformed. The music began in one key and moved to another as if on a kind of journey—a process of departure and metamorphosis—before returning. It was the musical equivalent of the tendency in Baroque architecture to design buildings so they would impart a sense of dramatic narrative to a visitor moving through their spaces. As one traveled through the changing curves and textures of rooms and hallways, encountered contrasts of large and small, noted the shifting qualities of light and shadow—these architectural elements worked, through the unfolding of time, to create an emotional climax. And so did the wandering themes and shifting key centers of the sonata.

Equal temperament was not, however, the only tuning proposed to accommodate this new musical trend. By 1681, a theorist named Andreas Werckmeister had developed an irregular tuning system that came to be known as "well temperament." In Werckmeister's well-tempered tuning, certain keys were more in tune than others, but none were so out of tune as to be unplayable. Therefore, as a musical work moved from one key center to another, the shift would become blatant: the more far-reaching the displacement, the more grating the harmonies. This variegation—a kind of perspective through audible shading—was seized upon as a good thing by opponents of equal temperament, who saw in Werckmeister's system the advantage of a built-in musical syntax. Changes in a piece's scales and harmonies were now overlaid with an added expressive element: a dramatic change in the quality of sound, depending on which tones the music revolved around at a given moment. (Of course, this change would only occur on keyboard instruments; strings and woodwinds were left to pursue their own musical grammars.)

Advocates claimed for well temperament the bonus of giving each key its own character; but for many, subjecting a keyboard to gradations of "in- and out-of-tuneness" offered little in the way of musical value. Indeed, Werckmeister himself eventually became an advocate for equal temperament. The German critic and composer Friedrich Wilhelm Marpurg—who, at the request of the heirs of Bach, wrote a preface for a new edition of the master's *Art of Fugue*—offered a terse critique of the well-tempered system in 1776: "Diversity in the character of the keys," he wrote, "will serve only to increase a 'diversity' of bad sounds in the performance."

There is controversy to this day over whether Bach preferred equal or well temperament. Some theorists contend that there is internal evidence in his music—differences in the way he handled different keys—to suggest he had well temperament in mind. (One modern scholar insists that he has broken the code of Bach's "secret tuning" by unraveling the images in the composer's personal seal, which contained seven points and five dashes. However, his secret solution conflicts with statements about temperament made by musicians in Bach's circle.) There is as much evidence on the other side: Bach's biographer Johann Nikolaus Forkel reported, for example, that Bach moved so subtly through the keys that listeners never noticed the change; this suggests equal temperament. His obituary made a similar comment about the artful way in which he tuned his instruments. What's more, as pianist Charles Rosen has pointed out, there are many cases in which Bach transposed the same material from one key to another, apparently without regard for the dramatic changes that would ensue in well-temperament.

Rameau's own advocacy of equal temperament came only after considerable reflection. It placed him at odds not only with Rousseau, but with many of the other important minds of his time. From the beginning, however, controversy seemed to be this man's calling. He developed a reputation early on for both abundant talent and explosive outbursts. At age twenty-three Rameau entered an organ contest for an important job, won against Antoine Dornel, one of the most renowned organists of Paris, and then refused the position. At thirty-two, unhappy at his post as organist at Clermont Cathedral, he noisily closed the organ and stormed out during morning services, and at later services created such a wild, cacophonous sound that a choirboy had to be sent to stop him. After moving to Paris, he often became embroiled in quarrels in the cafés. Yet, Voltaire could say with all sincerity, "My cold blood runs warm at the name of Rameau."

Those who knew the composer thought he looked quite a bit like his friend Voltaire: tall and thin, with "a sharp chin, no stomach, flutes for legs." He was, according to one report, "more like a ghost than a man," and one acquaintance, Friedrich Melchior von Grimm, reported that Rameau was "as emaciated and shriveled as M. de Voltaire." He must have been energetic, however: At forty-two, he married a girl of eighteen. In any event, looks aside, his music was ravishing.

Diderot described Rameau in his wild romp of a novel, *The*

Indiscreet Jewels (in which a magical ring compels the private parts of various women to reveal their secret histories). Here he is the unusual, brilliant, and learned Uremifasolasiututut, a composer before whom "no one had ever distinguished the delicate nuances that separate the tender from the voluptuous, the voluptuous from the passionate, the passionate from the lascivious." However, in *Rameau's Nephew*—Diderot's brilliant depiction of an unbridled genius colliding with the constraints of a civilized life—Rameau has become the famous musician "who wrote so much visionary gibberish and apocalyptic truth about the theory of music—writings that neither he nor anyone else ever understood."

Actually, only about half of what he wrote was gibberish. Rameau's earliest writings applied, for the first time, a scientific method to music, generating principles of harmonic movement that are still in use today. It was Rameau who first suggested that a chord built by stacking the tones *do, mi,* and *sol* is really the same as one that places *mi* on the bottom, *sol* in the middle, and *do* on top. He used both Descartes and Newton as models in a search for universal laws—describing the behavior of dissonance in mechanical terms, as colliding objects. And he developed a scientific theory of music based on the sonorous body—the fixed set of tones produced by any vibrating object, through which, he believed, nature herself imposed the rules of musical harmony.

The pursuit of nature's laws led him to a short-lived friendship with Father Louis-Bertrand Castel, inventor of the ocular harpsichord. Inspired by Descartes's theory of light, Castel tried to perfect a keyboard that would couple the sounding of pitches with the projection of colors (he equated certain tones with the colors blue, red, and yellow, and, following Rameau's musical treatise *Génération har-monique,* wrote of a *"génération harmonique des couleurs"*). Different attempts at building his instrument—some using paper strips, others colored glass—occupied Castel for some thirty years. (Technology and art continued to progress hand in hand. By the end of the eighteenth century, German scientist Johann Heinrich Lambert would propose an instrument by which people could enjoy music through their teeth, so as not to awaken others who are sleeping.)

Father Castel, in a review of Rameau's treatise on harmony, first brought to the composer's attention the existence of higher overtones emitted by vibrating strings. Apparently, Rameau had until then been unaware of this scientific fact, but its discovery only encouraged his theoretical approach. His *New System of Music Theory* in 1726 recognized the acoustical findings of Sauveur, and reasserted that all music stems from the natural action of a vibrating body which, by natural law, emits, in its first few overtones (the octave, third, and fifth), the "perfect chord." Given this unfailing acoustical law, musical expression, he explained, resulted from the natural inclinations of each harmony to move toward certain others—like a gravitational law of music.

The powerful effects that could be achieved by a master harmonist armed with this knowledge are described by Diderot in his *Leçons de clavecin* (Keyboard Lessons):

If you have a little imagination; if you can feel; if the sounds capture your soul; if you are born with a volatile disposition; if nature has chosen you to experience ecstasy for yourself and to transmit it to others, what will have happened to you [during the movement of

harmonies from one key to another]? [You will picture] a
man who awakens at the center of a labyrinth. There he
is searching left and right for an exit; one moment he
believed that he was reaching the end of his errors; he
stops, he follows with an uncertain and trembling step,
the route, deceptive perhaps, that opens before
him . . . he imagines a free place beyond a forest that he
proposes to cross; he runs; he rests; he runs again; he
climbs, he climbs; he has attained the summit of a hill;
he descends; he falls; he rises, bruised from falls and
refalls, he goes; he arrives, he looks, and he recognizes
the very place of his awakening.

By 1737, with the publication of *Génération harmonique,*
Rameau had concluded that music's evolving harmonic art
required equal temperament for its realization, and he
rejected mean-tone tuning. But his advocacy of the radical
tuning faced an uphill battle. The *Mercure de France* announced that a paper read to the Lyon Academy showed
that on temperament and tuning, "M. Rameau himself has
determined nothing." (Under Rameau's epistolary fire, the
presenter, Louis Bollioud-Mermet, recanted and professed to
have no quarrel with the composer's foundations for equal
temperament. He merely questioned whether musicians
whose ears are not "excellent and accustomed to tuning"
would be able to obtain equal temperament on their instruments, he said, and therefore offered for sale his own invention for that purpose, something he called the *phtongomètre.*)

Meanwhile, Rousseau continued to assail the supposed
scientific basis of Rameau's theories—and so did the scientists. Daniel Bernoulli pointed out that every vibrating body

contains a potentially infinite number of overtones. If you take an iron rod by the middle and strike it, said Bernoulli, you will hear a confused mix of unharmonious sounds. How could Rameau claim a natural basis for his "perfect chord"? Well, replied Rameau, strike a pair of suspended tongs. There will be a noisy clang at first, but it will quickly settle down to produce a harmonious sound. And "the lowest sound of the whole body" will begin to seize your attention. This is the fundamental bass of the sonorous body, the true compass of the ear.

In fact, he asserted, that's why equal temperament works. Although on the surface its altered proportions may appear to tarnish nature's perfect intervals, in truth equal temperament shows that the ear depends on this fundamental bass—the lowest tone of the sonorous body—to guide it. Once it perceives this foundation, it understands intuitively the relationships that are intended between the musical tones that sound above it.

It was, for a time, a reasoned dialogue. But Rameau was not content to stop there. He had crowned himself as "the only one who has written scientifically, good or bad, on music" since Zarlino. Now, he saw his concept of nature's sonorous body as the basis of all mathematics, and of metaphysics too. The idea of the sonorous body became for him—in the midst of the Enlightenment, a movement that claimed to value reason above all!—a symbol of divine revelation. Rameau claimed that ancient Egyptian priests had secretly treasured it; that it was the source of Chinese and Greek music; that Noah carried knowledge of the sonorous body with him on the ark, and that his sons had brought it to the four corners of the earth.

This did little to help his cause. Rousseau countered that any system based on science, "no matter how ingenious . . . is not at all based on nature . . . it was only established on some analogies or convergences that can be overturned tomorrow by an inventive man who finds more natural ones." Even d'Alembert, who had done Rameau the favor of presenting his theories in a simplified version with the book *Elémens de musique théorique et pratique,* tried to remind him that as a theorist it was important to recognize shades of certainty rather than black-and-white truths. "The supreme Intelligence has drawn a veil before our feeble vision which we try in vain to remove," he wrote to his friend. "It is a sad lot for our curiosity and our pride, but it is the lot of humanity."

Rameau was unrelenting. By the end of his life he had severed most of his friendships, and continued down his own, narrow path. Rousseau, taking his antisocietal ideas to their farthest extremes, also relinquished many of his relationships. He left Paris for a house in the mountains.

Nevertheless, the contributions and influence of each were undeniable. Rameau was "the first to have made music a science worthy of the attention of philosophers," wrote d'Alembert, "to have simplified the practice of it and made it easier, to have taught musicians to use reasoning and analogy." What's more, he connected the deepest yearnings of his age—for freedom of thought and expression—to musical art. "I am astonished in a century where so many authors occupy themselves writing about freedom of trade, freedom of marriage, freedom of the press, and freedom in art, that nobody thus far has written about freedom in music," noted d'Alembert. "For all freedoms are bound together and are

The Triumph of Rameau, an anonymous etching

equally dangerous. Freedom in music implies freedom to feel, freedom to feel implies freedom to think, freedom to think implies freedom to act . . ." If one wants to protect the state, suggested d'Alembert (mimicking Plato), it is important to keep music from changing. Certainly, it was too late for that.

In 1749, the register of the Academie Royale des Sciences in Paris reported that Jean-Philippe Rameau's support of equal temperament was cause for serious consideration. During a lifetime of debate, he managed to convince many others of its possibilities as well. Indeed, his revolutionary approach to music theory and its artistic implications edged the next generations toward equal temperament's inevitable adoption.

Seven years after Rameau's recognition by the Parisian academy, Wolfgang Amadeus Mozart was born in Salzburg, Austria. Mozart's sublime musicality and the rapturous ease with which he created a classic ideal of beauty set a standard for a new artistic era—one that placed a high value on symmetry, transparency, and grace. Many adherents of that late-eighteenth-century model—including important musical figures such as Georg Joseph Vogler, Daniel Gottlob Türk, and Mozart's student, Johann Nepomuk Hummel—nudged the door open even wider for the easy constancy of "Rameau's tuning" as well as for the new expressiveness of the piano. Though other, unequal tunings continued to circulate—and to find substantial support—equal temperament was here to stay. And music would never be the same.

14

Coda

Hefts of the moving world at innocent gambols silently
    rising, freshly exuding,
Scooting obliquely high and low.

                   —Walt Whitman, "Song of Myself"

The change was gradual. Meantone tuning continued to be used on many organs throughout the nineteenth century; for acoustical reasons, equal temperament's impure thirds sound much coarser on organ pipes than they do on piano strings. And piano technicians continued to face practical difficulties in achieving an equal division of the octave; there were some who still found it undesirable.

In truth, equal temperament is actually impossible to attain even on today's pianos. A modern piano's strings are in a condition of permanent out-of-tuneness known as *inharmonicity*. Such factors as stiffness, width, temperature, humidity and rust all exert an influence in this direction; a further complication arises from the fact that the various materials used in the construction of musical instruments each contribute different resonating properties. All these stand in the way of a perfect tuning. Indeed, inside a contemporary grand piano there are places where a single hammer strikes two or three strings simultaneously in order to amplify the sound of a single tone, and those paired strings never produce a true unison—the sound is fuller, and more characteristic of a piano, when they don't. Tuning is still an art governed by the ear, not the slide rule. It will always be so.

Nevertheless, with Rameau's help, the temperament wars, after centuries of struggle, had essentially reached an end. Despite the technical challenges that remained, equal temperament settled in as the *philosophical ideal*. And it made all the difference in the world.

Over the next centuries, Beethoven and Schubert, Liszt and Chopin continued to dissolve the limits of musical form, producing art that would not have been possible with any other tuning. At the turn of the twentieth century, impressionists and expressionists took advantage of equal temperament's harmonic pliancy, painting musical portraits free of references to a particular tonal center. By 1923 Arnold Schoenberg began using his twelve-tone system of composition with the aim of eliminating the distinction between consonance and dissonance altogether. Schoenberg put an end to the very idea of natural law in music. Each tone in his system became an equal entity governed only by the hierarchy imposed by an individual composer.

The piano evolved and proliferated. By the mid–nineteenth century, there were more than three hundred piano makers in England alone. In 1868, Paris boasted more than twenty thousand piano teachers. Soon, the piano craze spread to other regions of the world—brought by covered wagons to log cabins on America's western frontier, and by

The Steinway overstrung piano

camels to Arabia. As the twentieth century began, Americans were buying more than 350,000 pianos a year. And they were all tuned, more or less, in equal temperament.

Iron frames replaced wooden ones, creating a more brilliant instrument, and this was followed by other innovations. In the United States, Steinway & Sons introduced the overstrung square piano in 1855 (a new, more practical design in which the bass strings cross over the treble), and in 1859, the overstrung grand. Within years, this single piano maker would garner more than 120 patents for changes and improvements to the old designs, creating an instrument with a power and nuance unimagined in the eighteenth century.

Today's piano is a miraculous machine: a colossus of cast iron and wood—filled with screws, hammers, and felt—weighing nearly a thousand pounds. Its frame sustains twenty-two tons of tension exerted on its strings—the equivalent of twenty medium-sized cars. Yet it can respond to the slightest whisper of a pianist's touch, producing a sound as warm and caressing as the human voice. Concertgoers the world over still flock to hear its magical sounds, unaware of the long controversy that once brewed over the way its tones are arranged, in twelve equal steps within each octave. For most, the idea that they might be formulated another way has simply never arisen.

Yet the temperament debate never completely disappeared. Even in the twenty-first century, a sense of intrigue and excitement over the ancient tunings keeps the topic burning with partisan heat. It is particularly fertile ground for early-music specialists, of course. But there is also plenty of action in other quarters.

Musicologist Ernest G. McClain, in books such as *The Myth of Invariance,* probes what he sees as hidden musical meanings in the texts of the world's religions, from the Rig-Veda and the Egyptian Book of the Dead to the Book of Revelation. McClain, in his retirement years, invests a tremendous amount of time and effort pursuing what he calls "Davidic musicology" (named for the biblical David). "It's a little astonishing to attribute temperament theory to someone who lived in 1000 B.C.E.," he admits. But he cites evidence in the Bible, in the Sumerian Kings list, and in Babylonian legend of a very early awareness of the mathematical calculations used for a range of musical proportions. "The oldest stories we have of gods and heroes are really about music," he says.

Contemporary composers who place temperament at the core of their work include Lou Harrison—who has employed the tunings of Johann Philipp Kirnberger, a student of Bach who was decidedly against equal temperament—and distinguished composer and scholar Easley Blackwood, a longtime professor at the University of Chicago. Blackwood has written music using a variety of equal temperaments, dividing the octave up into from thirteen to twenty-four slices. These "microtonal" works are stunningly strange—sometimes edgy and dark, at other times brightly boisterous, often haunting and otherworldly.

A flourishing circle of just-intonation advocates with ties to Eastern mysticism includes clusters of adherents in New York and California. One is W. A. Mathieu, whose mammoth book *Harmonic Experience* explores music's inner workings and its resonance with human experience. Mathieu, who first became known as a jazz musician, studied with Blackwood, whom he credits with imparting important mathematical insights into the nature of temperament. "Then I heard Northern Indian music," he relates, "and found in it a kind of purity that I longed for but couldn't achieve or understand." He studied under Indian master musician Pandit Pran Nath, became friends with innovative composer Terry Riley, and developed his own approach to the similarities and differences between pure and equal-tempered tunings.

"Each one is a complete universe unto itself," he explains, "but they own mutual territory. Equal temperament is not a substitute for just intonation, just as adulthood is not a substitute for childhood. You could say that just intonation is like the pure child that lives inside every equal-tempered adult." In his view (and it comes close to Rameau's), the tonal world of equal temperament brings with it the kind of ambiguity that manages to fool the ears into thinking they are hearing pure ratios. But, says Mathieu, we are actually built to resonate with the pure musical proportions. "Human beings don't have to know about just intonation to understand it," he says. "We already *are* it."

New York pianist and composer Michael Harrison also studied with Pandit Pran Nath, and worked extensively with composer La Monte Young, becoming the first person besides Young to perform that composer's six-hour just-intonation work, *The Well-Tuned Piano*. Harrison converted a seven-foot grand piano into an instrument he calls the "harmonic piano," which affords him, with the shift of a pedal, the ability to play up to twenty-four different notes per octave. There are also devices for controlling which strings are free to vibrate sympathetically. In 1991 he used this instrument to record an album, *From Ancient Worlds*.

One cold evening at the end of November 1999, I was invited to Harrison's brownstone for a private recital. Earlier in the month, he had participated in a festival in Rome as one of four composer/pianists in the minimalist mode—a style of writing in which brief, repeating melodic fragments undergo a process of change over time, like precious stones turned slowly under a light. The other pianists on the program were Philip Glass, Terry Riley, and Charlemagne Palestine. The morning after his recital, Harrison awoke with a new tuning in mind—he calls it his "revelation tuning." It had come to him clearly, like a revelation, he reported. When he returned home and tried it on his harmonic piano, he found the results extraordinary: "It creates undulating waves of pulsating sonic energy," he later related. "It is a tuning of so many beautiful sounds that every time I play it I discover new harmonic regions and feel like an explorer." The secret, he revealed, was the inclusion in the tuning of three commas—those tiny "wolf" intervals that are usually avoided as too sour. He had found a way to weave them into a unique tapestry of sound.

The private recital at his home was an opportunity for Harrison to play his new tuning for a few friends and musicians, including composer Philip Glass. Glass, an icon of contemporary music whose credits include several operas, such as *Einstein on the Beach* and *Satyagraha,* and collaborations with poet Allen Ginsberg and pop artists Paul Simon, David Byrne, and Laurie Anderson, arrived with a retinue. We all shared some wine and small talk before descending to a basement room, the locus of which was a glistening, ebony harmonic piano. The floor was strewn with cushions, and we each quickly settled onto one. Glass found a couch at the far end of the room and assumed a cross-legged position. And then, in the dim light, the music began.

It sounded like a jumble at first—a drone, or a room full of drones. Then, from within the din, high-pitched sounds seemed to rise and float toward the ceiling. The deeper Harrison played into the bass end of the instrument, the more he seemed to free an angelic choir above. Were these sympathetic vibrations? I wondered. Overtones? The clashing of strings just slightly out of tune? I couldn't tell.

Now the texture changed. The pianist's fingers engaged in a furious rhythmic interplay, and a groaning mass of sound in the low end of the piano gave birth to more phantoms above. Musical concords seemed to emerge and shake hands above the fray.

After a considerable amount of time, the music stopped. No one moved. Someone on the floor said, "My whole body is resonating." The piano was silent, but we were all still spinning in a musical vortex. I looked at Glass on the couch; his eyes were closed. My mind wandered to the lamps in the room, the decorations on the walls. . . .

And then I thought fleetingly of Renaissance seekers like Bartolomeo Ramos and Marsilio Ficino and Pico della Mirandola. I remembered the kabbalistic masters who described the sympathetic resonance between what is above and what is below. I contemplated the curious story of Huai Nan Tzu, his temperament theories and his ascent to heaven.

And I once again recalled the latest trend in modern physics, known as string theory, which holds that everything in the universe is composed not of atoms, but of infinitely thin vibrating strings—filaments that wriggle and oscillate incessantly in a great cosmic dance. What were once described as different elementary particles are, say physicists, really just different notes in an enormous celestial symphony.

And I thought: Perhaps Pythagoras was right after all.

Acknowledgments

The list of people to whom I owe a debt of gratitude upon the completion of this book is not quite endless, but it nearly seems so. To begin, there are the many scholars whose works I found simply indispensable. These include historians Will and Ariel Durant, art scholar Erwin Panofsky, musicologists Murray Barbour, H. F. Cohen, Mark Lindley, Edward E. Lowinsky, Claude Palisca, Emanuel Winternitz, and the Italian temperament specialist Patrizio Barbieri, who generously shared many of his writings with me. In addition, the editors of and contributors to *The New Grove Dictionary of Music and Musicians* have my undying appreciation.

I am extremely lucky to count among my friends the inventor Liam Comerford and his colleague at IBM the mathematician and physicist Raimo Bakis; pianist and polymath Steven Lubin; Laurence Libin and Stewart Pollens, both musical curators at New York's Metropolitan Museum of Art; and musician and theorist W. A. Mathieu. Their counsel meant more to me than I can say.

The project would never have seen the light of day without the expert help and enthusiastic guidance of my editor, Jonathan Segal, and my agent, Mel Berger, both of whom believed in it right from the start. Thanks are due also to many libraries—Cambridge University Library; the Royal Society in London; Debby Benz and Virginia Fetscher of the Katonah Public Library; Ruth Rando of the Closter Public Library; and Jane Gottlieb of the Juilliard School of Music Library—and to Maxine and Dr. Frank Brady and Frank's colleague at St. John's University, philosopher Michael Henry; pianists Riccardo

Acknowledgments

Scivales, Douglas Riva, Joseph Bloch, Michael Harrison, and Olli Mustonen (as well as Olli's father, Sepo Mustonen, a professor of statistics at the University of Helsinki); harpsichordist Ed Brewer; translators Robert Cowan, Francesca Magnani, and Dr. Debra Popkin; kabbalah scholar Elliot Wolfson; Kent Webb, John Patton, and Leo Spellman of Steinway & Sons; Ida Giragossian of Alfred A. Knopf; scientists Stephanie Pfirman and Peter Schlosser; illustrator Art Glazer; Angela Duryea; John Aslan; scientist Frederick G. Reinagel and my friend and longtime employer, Ed Shanaphy. Any errors of fact or interpretation are, of course, entirely mine. Mentions are also due my Tai Chi teacher, Ed Young, who helps me stay rooted to the ground, and my gymnastics instructor, Randy Pendergrast, who taught me how to take flight.

Last but not least are the members of my family. My brother, Dr. Mark Isacoff, has always offered unconditional support for my every endeavor, and this project was no exception. Heartfelt thanks go to my mother and father for a lifetime of nurturing. Finally, for my wife and daughters, no words could possibly suffice; to them this book is lovingly dedicated.

Bibliography

Abraham, Gerald, editor. *The New Oxford History of Music,* Volume IV: *The Age of Humanism, 1540–1630.* London: Oxford University Press, 1968.

Aczel, Amir D. *Fermat's Last Theorem.* New York: Four Walls Eight Windows, 1996.

Aeschylus. *Agamemnon,* translated by Richmond Lattimore, in *Greek Tragedies,* Volume 1, David Grene and Richmond Lattimore, editors. Chicago: Phoenix Books, 1962.

Alberti, Leon Battista. *On Painting,* translated by John R. Spencer. New Haven and London: Yale University Press, 1966.

Apel, Willi. *The History of Keyboard Music to 1700,* translated and revised by Hans Tischler. Bloomington and London: Indiana University Press, 1972.

Auden, W. H. *Selected Poems,* Edward Mendelson, editor. New York: Vintage Books, 1979.

Avery, Charles, and David Finn. *Bernini.* New York: Little, Brown and Company, 1997.

Bach, C. P. E. *Essay on the True Art of Playing Keyboard Instruments,* translated by William J. Mitchell. New York and London: W. W. Norton, 1949.

Barbera, André, translator. *The Euclidean Division of the Canon.* Lincoln and London: University of Nebraska Press, 1991.

Barbieri, Patrizio. *Strumenti per Mozart.* Milan: Istituto per la Ricerca Organologica, 1991.

Bibliography

Barbour, J. Murray. *Tuning and Temperament: A Historical Survey.* East Lansing: Michigan State College Press, 1951.

Baxandall, Michael. *Painting and Experience in Fifteenth Century Italy.* London: Oxford University Press, 1972.

Bazin, Germain. *A History of Art,* translated by Francis Scarge. London: Thames and Hudson, 1968.

Benade, Arthur H. *Fundamentals of Musical Acoustics.* Mineola, N.Y.: Dover Publications, 1990.

Bicknell, Stephen. *The History of the English Organ.* Cambridge: Cambridge University Press, 1996.

Blackwood, Easley. *The Structure of Recognizable Diatonic Tunings.* Princeton: Princeton University Press, 1985.

Blume, Friedrich. *Renaissance and Baroque Music.* New York: W. W. Norton, 1967.

Boase, T. S. R. *Giorgio Vasari: The Man and the Book.* Princeton: Princeton University Press, 1979.

Bonfil, Robert. *Jewish Life in Renaissance Italy,* translated by Anthony Oldcorn. Berkeley and Los Angeles: University of California Press, 1991.

Bossy, John. *Giordano Bruno and the Embassy Affair.* New Haven and London: Yale University Press, 1991.

Bowles, Paul. *The Thicket of Spring.* Los Angeles: Black Sparrow Press, 1972.

Bowra, C. M. *The Greek Experience.* New York: New American Library, 1963.

Braudel, Fernand. *The Structures of Everyday Life,* translated by Siân Reynolds. New York: Harper & Row, 1981.

Bréhier, Emile. *The Hellenic Age,* translated by Joseph Thomas. Chicago and London: University of Chicago Press, 1963.

Brewer, John. *The Pleasures of the Imagination: English Culture in the Eighteenth Century.* New York: Farrar, Straus, Giroux, 1997.

Brown, Howard Mayer. *Embellishing Sixteenth Century Music.* New York: Oxford University Press, 1976.

———. *Music in the Renaissance.* Englewood Cliffs, N.J.: Prentice-Hall, 1976.

Burton, Robert. *The Anatomy of Melancholy,* edited by Floyd Dell and Paul Jordan-Smith. New York: Tudor Publishing Company, 1951.

Bibliography

The Cambridge Modern History. New York: MacMillan Company, 1934.

Careri, Giovanni. *Bernini: Flights of Love, the Art of Devotion.* Chicago: University of Chicago Press, 1995.

Carpenter, Nan Cooke. *Music in the Medieval and Renaissance Universities.* New York: Da Capo Press, 1972.

Cassirer, Ernst, Paul Oskar Kristeller, John Herman Randall, Jr., editors. *The Renaissance Philosophy of Man.* Chicago: Phoenix Books, 1948.

Christensen, Thomas. *Rameau and Musical Thought in the Enlightenment.* Cambridge: Cambridge University Press, 1993.

Christianson, Gale E. *In the Presence of the Creator: Isaac Newton and His Times.* New York: Free Press, 1984.

Coelho, Victor, editor. *Music and Science in the Age of Galileo.* Dordrecht: Kluwer Academic Publishers, 1992.

Cohen, H. F. *Quantifying Music: The Science of Music in the First Stage of the Scientific Revolution, 1580–1650.* Dordrecht: Reidel, 1984.

Cohen, I. Bernard. *Revolution in Science.* Cambridge: Belknap Press of Harvard University Press, 1985.

Cowart, Georgia, editor. *French Musical Thought, 1600–1800.* Ann Arbor: UMI Research Press, 1989.

Crane, Milton, editor. *Fifty Great Poets.* New York: Bantam Books, Inc., 1968.

Croix, Horst de la, and Richard G. Tansey. *Gardner's Art Through the Ages.* New York: Harcourt, Brace & World, Inc., 1970.

Crosby, Alfred W. *The Measure of Reality.* Cambridge: Cambridge University Press, 1997.

Crowther, J. G. *Founders of British Science.* London: Cresset Press, 1960.

Cru, R. Loyalty, Ph.D. *Diderot as a Disciple of English Thought.* New York: AMS Press, 1966.

Dantzig, Tobias. *Number, the Language of Science.* New York: Macmillan, 1958.

Daston, Lorraine, and Katharine Park. *Wonders and the Order of Nature, 1150–1750.* New York: Zone Books, 1998.

David, Hans T., and Arthur Mendel, editors. *The New Bach Reader: A Life of Johann Sebastian Bach in Letters and Documents,* revised by Christoph Wolff. New York and London: W. W. Norton, 1998.

Bibliography

Denis, Jean. *Treatise on Harpsichord Tuning,* translated by Vincent J. Panetta Jr. Cambridge: Cambridge University Press, 1987.

Descartes, René. *Compendium of Music,* translated by Walter Robert. Leawood, Kans.: American Institute of Musicology, 1961.

———. *Oeuvres,* edited by Charles Adam and Paul Tannery. Paris: Librairie Philosophique J. Vrin, 1974.

———. *The Essential Writings,* translated by John J. Blom. New York: Harper & Row, 1977.

———. *The Philosophical Writings of Descartes,* Volume III, *The Correspondence,* translated by John Cottingham, Robert Stoothoff, Dugald Murdoch, and Anthony Kenny. Cambridge: Cambridge University Press, 1991.

Diderot, Denis. *Diderot on Art,* Volume I, edited and translated by John Goodman. New Haven and London: Yale University Press, 1995.

———. *The Indiscreet Jewels,* translated by Sophie Hawkes. New York: Marsilio Publishers, 1993.

———. *Rameau's Nephew,* translated by Jacques Barzun. Indianapolis: Bobbs-Merrill Company, Inc., 1956.

Dobbs, Betty Jo Teeter. *The Foundations of Newton's Alchemy.* Cambridge: Cambridge University Press, 1975.

Dodds, E. R. *The Greeks and the Irrational.* Berkeley and Los Angeles: University of California Press, 1965.

Duffy, Eamon. *Saints and Sinners.* New Haven: Yale University Press, 1997.

Durant, Will. *The Age of Faith.* New York: Simon and Schuster, 1950.

———. *The Reformation.* New York: Simon and Schuster, 1957.

———. *The Renaissance.* New York: Simon and Schuster, 1953.

Durant, Will and Ariel. *The Age of Louis XIV.* New York: Simon and Schuster, 1963.

———. *The Age of Reason Begins.* New York: Simon and Schuster, 1961.

———. *The Age of Voltaire.* New York: Simon and Schuster, 1965.

Eimerl, Sarel. *The World of Giotto, c. 1267–1337.* New York: Time-Life Books, 1967.

Encyclopedia Judaica. Jerusalem: Keter Publishing House, 1972.

Bibliography

Encyclopedia of World Art. London: McGraw-Hill Book Company, 1960.

'Espinasse, Margaret. *Robert Hooke.* Berkeley and Los Angeles: University of California Press, 1962.

Euclid. *The Thirteen Books of Euclid's Elements,* translated by Sir Thomas L. Heath. New York: Dover Publications, 1956.

Farrington, Benjamin. *Greek Science.* Baltimore: Penguin Books, 1966.

Fauvel, John, Raymond Flood, Michael Shortland, Robin Wilson, editors. *Let Newton Be.* Oxford: Oxford University Press, 1988.

Ficino, Marsilio, *Meditations on the Soul.* Rochester, Vt.: Inner Traditions, 1997.

Friedlaender, Walter. *Mannerism and Anti-Mannerism in Italian Painting.* New York: Schocken Books, 1965.

Galilei, Galileo. *Discoveries and Opinions of Galileo,* translated by Stillman Drake. Garden City: Doubleday, 1957.

Gallo, F. Alberto. *Music of the Middle Ages,* Volume II, translated by Karen Eales. Cambridge: Cambridge University Press, 1985.

Gardner, John. *The Life and Times of Chaucer.* New York: Vintage Books, 1978.

Gaukroger, Stephen. *Descartes: An Intellectual Biography.* Oxford: Clarendon Press, 1995.

Girdlestone, Cuthbert. *Jean-Philippe Rameau: His Life and Work.* New York: Dover Publications, 1969.

Gould, Stephen Jay. *Leonardo's Mountain of Clams and the Diet of Worms.* New York: Harmony Books, 1998.

Grant, Michael. *The Rise of the Greeks.* New York: Charles Scribner's Sons, 1987.

Greene, Brian. *The Elegant Universe.* New York: W. W. Norton & Company, 1999.

Grout, Donald Jay. *A History of Western Music.* New York: W. W. Norton, 1960.

Hale, John. *The Civilization of Europe in the Renaissance.* New York: Atheneum, 1994.

Hall, A. Rupert. *From Galileo to Newton.* New York: Harper & Row, 1963.

Bibliography

————. *The Scientific Revolution, 1500–1800: The Formation of the Modern Scientific Attitude.* Boston: Beacon Press, 1966.

Hall, David L., and Roger T. Ames. *Thinking from the Han: Self, Truth, and Transcendence in Chinese and Western Culture.* Albany: State University of New York Press, 1998.

Hamlin, Talbot. *Architecture Through the Ages.* New York: G. P. Putnam's Sons, 1953.

Heer, Friedrich. *The Medieval World.* Cleveland: World Publishing Company, 1961.

Hollander, John. *The Untuning of the Sky: Ideas of Music in English Poetry, 1500–1700.* New York: W. W. Norton, 1970.

Hoppin, Richard H. *Medieval Music.* New York: W. W. Norton & Company, 1978.

Huntley, H. E. *The Divine Proportion: A Study of Mathematical Beauty.* New York: Dover Publications, 1970.

Huygens, Christiaan. *Le Cycle Harmonique; Novus Cyclus Harmonicus,* edited by Rudolf Rasch. Utrecht: Diapason Press, 1986.

Hyman, Isabelle, editor. *Brunelleschi in Perspective.* Englewood Cliffs, N.J.: Prentice-Hall, Inc., 1974.

James, Jamie. *The Music of the Spheres.* New York: Copernicus, 1995.

Jorgensen, Owen H. *Tuning: Containing the Perfection of Eighteenth-Century Temperament, the Lost Art of Nineteenth-Century Temperament and the Science of Equal Temperament.* East Lansing: Michigan State University Press, 1991.

Keane, Sister Michaela Maria. *The Theoretical Writings of Jean-Philippe Rameau.* Washington, D.C.: Catholic University of America Press, 1961.

Kepler, Johannes. *The Harmonies of the World,* Great Books of the Western World, ed. Robert Hutchins. Chicago: Encyclopaedia Britannica, 1952.

Kirnberger, Johann Philipp. *The Art of Strict Musical Composition,* translated by David Beach and Jurgen Thym. New Haven and London: Yale University Press, 1982.

Kitto, H. D. F. *The Greeks.* Baltimore: Penguin Books, 1965.

Koestler, Arthur. *The Watershed: A Biography of Johannes Kepler.* Garden City, N.Y.: Anchor Books, 1960.

Bibliography

Kristeller, Paul Oskar. *Renaissance Thought: The Classic, Scholastic, and Humanist Strains.* New York: Harper Torchbooks, 1961.

Kuttner, Fritz A. *The Archeology of Music in Ancient China.* New York: Paragon House, 1990.

Larner, John. *Marco Polo and the Discovery of the World.* New Haven and London: Yale University Press, 1999.

Lasserre, Pierre. *The Spirit of French Music,* translated by Denis Turner. New York: E. P. Dutton & Co., 1921.

Lau, D. C., and Roger T. Ames, translators. *Yuan Dao: Tracing Dao to Its Source.* New York: Ballantine Books, 1998.

Lavin, Irving, editor. *Gianlorenzo Bernini: New Aspects of His Art and Thought.* University Park and London: Pennsylvania State University Press, 1985.

Le Blanc, Charles. *Huai-Nan Tzu: Philosophical Synthesis in Early Han Thought.* Hong Kong: Hong Kong University Press, 1985.

Lindley, Mark. *Lutes, Viols and Temperaments.* Cambridge: Cambridge University Press, 1984.

Lippman, Edward A. editor. *Musical Aesthetics: A Historical Reader,* Volume 1. New York: Pendragon Press, 1986.

Lloyd, Lt. S., and Hugh Boyle. *Intervals, Scales and Temperaments.* London: Macdonald, 1963.

Lorris, Guillaume de, and Jean de Meun. *The Romance of the Rose,* translated by Charles Dahlberg. Hanover: University Press of New England, 1986.

Lowinsky, Edward E. *Music in the Culture of the Renaissance and Other Essays,* Bonnie J. Blackburn, editor. Chicago: University of Chicago Press, 1989.

Lowinsky, Edward E. *Adrian Willaert's Chromatic "Duo" Re-Examined.* Utrecht: Instituut voor Muziekwetenshap [after 1957].

Manchester, William. *A World Lit Only by Fire: The Medieval Mind and the Renaissance.* Boston: Little, Brown and Company, 1992.

Manetti, Antonio. *The Life of Brunelleschi,* translated by Catherine Enggass. University Park and London: Pennsylvania State University Press, 1970.

Manuel, Frank E. *A Portrait of Isaac Newton.* Cambridge: Belknap Press of Harvard University Press, 1968.

Bibliography

Marshall, David. *The Surprising Effects of Sympathy.* Chicago: University of Chicago Press, 1988.

Mathieu, W. A. *Harmonic Experience.* Rochester, Vt.: Inner Traditions International, 1997.

McClain, Ernest G. *The Myth of Invariance.* New York: Nicolas Hays, Ltd., 1976.

Mei, Girolamo. *Letters on Ancient and Modern Music,* annotated by Claude V. Palisca. Leawood, Kans.: American Institute of Musicology, 1960.

Mersenne, P. Marin. *Correspondance,* annotated by Cornelis de Waard. Paris: Editions du Centre National de la Recherche Scientifique, 1965.

Michel, Paul Henri. *The Cosmology of Giordano Bruno.* Ithaca: Cornell University Press, 1973.

Murdoch, Iris. *The Fire and the Sun: Why Plato Banished the Artists.* Oxford: Clarendon Press, 1977.

Murray, Peter and Linda Murray. *The Art of the Renaissance.* New York and Washington: Frederick A. Praeger, 1966.

Neuwirth, Erich. *Musical Temperaments.* New York and Vienna: Springer, 1997.

Newman, James R. editor. *Men and Numbers.* New York: Simon and Schuster, 1956.

Newton, Sir Isaac. *Mathematical Principles of Natural Philosophy.* Encyclopaedia Britannica, Inc., 1934.

———. "Treatise on Musical Temperament," unpublished, in the collection of Cambridge University Library.

O'Brien, Grant. *Ruckers: A Harpsichord and Virginal Building Tradition.* Cambridge: Cambridge University Press, 1990.

O'Kelly, Bernard, editor. *The Renaissance Image of Man and the World.* Columbus: Ohio State University Press, 1966.

Page, Christopher. *Discarding Images.* Oxford: Clarendon Press, 1993.

———. *The Owl and the Nightingale: Musical Life and Ideas in France, 1100–1300.* London: J. M. Dent, 1989.

Palisca, Claude V. *The Florentine Camerata.* New Haven: Yale University Press, 1989.

———. *Girolamo Mei: Letters on Ancient and Modern Music. A Study.* Leawood, Kans.: American Institute of Musicology, 1960.

Bibliography

Panofsky, Erwin. *The Codex Huygens and Leonardo da Vinci's Art Theory.* Westport, Conn.: Greenwood Press, 1971.

Partridge, Eric. *Origins.* New York: Macmillan Publishing Co., 1977.

Perkins, Leeman L. *Music in the Age of the Renaissance.* New York: W. W. Norton, 1999.

Pollens, Stewart. *The Early Pianoforte.* Cambridge: Cambridge University Press, 1995.

Pound, Ezra. *Shih-Ching: The Classic Anthology Defined by Confucius.* Cambridge: Harvard University Press, 1954.

Power, Eileen. *Medieval People.* New York: Barnes & Noble, 1966.

Quennell, C. H. B. and Marjorie. *Everyday Things in Ancient Greece.* G. P. Putnam's Sons, New York, 1960.

Rabb, Theodore K. editor. *The Thirty Years' War.* Boston: D. C. Heath and Company, 1964.

Rameau, Jean-Philippe. *Treatise on Harmony,* translated by Philip Gossett. New York: Dover Publications, 1971.

Robinson, Kenneth. *A Critical Study of Chu Tsai-yü's Contribution to the Theory of Equal Temperament in Chinese Music.* Wiesbaden: Fran Steiner Verlag, 1980.

Rodis-Lewis, Geneviève. *Descartes: His Life and Thought,* translated by Jane Marie Todd. Ithaca and London: Cornell University Press, 1995.

Rhys, Hedley Howell, editor. *Seventeenth Century Science and the Arts.* Princeton: Princeton University Press, 1961.

Rhodios, Apollonios. *The Argonautika: The Story of Jason and the Quest for the Golden Fleece,* translated by Peter Green. Berkeley: University of California Press, 1997.

Roth, Harold D. *Original Tao: Inward Training and the Foundations of Taoist Mysticism.* New York: Columbia University Press, 1999.

Rousseau, Jean-Jacques. *The Confessions,* translated by J. M. Cohen. London: Penguin Books, 1953.

Russell, Bertrand. *A History of Western Philosophy.* New York: Simon and Schuster, 1966.

Sadie, Stanley, editor. *The New Grove Dictionary of Music and Musicians.* London: Macmillan Publishers Ltd., 1980.

Sauveur, Joseph. *Collected Writings on Musical Acoustics (Paris 1700–1713),* edited by Rudolf Rasch. Utrecht: Diapason Press, 1984.

Bibliography

Schrade, Leo. *Monteverdi, Creator of Modern Music.* New York: W. W. Norton, 1950.

Schrade, Leo, editor. *Polyphonic Music of the Fourteenth Century,* Volume IV, *The Works of Francesco Landini.* Monaco: Editions de l'Oiseau-Lyre [after 1956].

Seay, Albert. *Music in the Medieval World.* Englewood Cliffs: Prentice-Hall, 1965.

Seward, Desmond. *Caravaggio: A Passionate Life.* New York: William Morrow and Company, Inc., 1998.

Siepmann, Jeremy. *The Piano.* London: David Campbell Publishers Ltd., 1996.

Simson, Otto von. *The Gothic Cathedral.* New York: Pantheon Books, 1956.

Singh, Simon. *Fermat's Enigma.* New York: Walker and Company, 1997.

Sobel, Dava. *Longitude.* New York: Walker and Company, 1995.

Stevens, Wallace, *Collected Poetry and Prose.* New York: Library of America, 1997.

Stewart, Ian. *Nature's Numbers.* New York: Basic Books, 1995.

Strohm, Reinhard. *The Rise of European Music, 1380–1500.* Cambridge: Cambridge University Press, 1993.

Stromberg, Roland N. *An Intellectual History of Modern Europe.* New York: Appleton-Century-Crofts, 1966.

Strunk, Oliver, editor. *The Baroque Era.* New York and London: W. W. Norton, 1965.

———. *The Renaissance.* New York and London: W. W. Norton, 1965.

Sullivan, Lawrence E. *Enchanting Powers: Music in the World's Religions.* Cambridge, Mass.: Harvard University Press, 1997.

Swift, Jonathan. *Gulliver's Travels,* Christopher Fox, editor. Boston: Bedford Books of St. Martin's Press, 1995.

Tomlinson, Gary. *Monteverdi and the End of the Renaissance.* Berkeley: University of California Press, 1987.

———. *Music in Renaissance Magic: Toward a Historiography of Others.* Chicago and London: University of Chicago Press, 1993.

Tuchman, Barbara W. *A Distant Mirror: The Calamitous Fourteenth Century.* New York: Ballantine Books, 1978.

Valens, Evans G. *The Number of Things.* New York: E. P. Dutton, 1964.

Bibliography

Vallentin, Antonina. *Leonardo Da Vinci,* translated by E. W. Dickes. New York: Viking Press, 1938.

Vasari, Giorgio. *The Great Masters,* translated by Gaston Du C. de Vere, Michael Sonino, editor. New York: Hugh Lauter Levin Associates, Inc., 1986.

Verba, Cynthia. *Music and the French Enlightenment.* Oxford: Clarendon Press, 1993.

Walker, D. P. *Studies in Musical Science in the Late Renaissance.* Leiden: E. J. Brill, 1978.

Watkins, Glenn. *Gesualdo: The Man and his Music.* Chapel Hill: University of North Carolina Press, 1976.

Werckmeister, Andreas. *Musicalische Temperatur* (1691), Rudolf Rasch, editor. Utrecht: Diapason Press, 1983.

Werner, Stephen. *Socratic Satire: An Essay on Diderot and "Le Neveu de Rameau."* Birmingham: Summa Publications, Inc., 1987.

White, Michael. *Isaac Newton: The Last Sorcerer.* Reading, Penn.: Helix Books, 1997.

Wiener, Philip P. editor. *Dictionary of the History of Ideas.* New York: Charles Scribner's Sons, 1973.

Wilson, Arthur M. *Diderot.* New York: Oxford University Press, 1972.

Winternitz, Emanuel. *Leonardo da Vinci as a Musician.* New Haven and London: Yale University Press, 1982.

Wolfe, Thomas. *Of Time and the River.* New York: Charles Scribner's Sons, 1935.

Yates, Frances A. *Giordano Bruno and the Hermetic Tradition.* Chicago: University of Chicago Press, 1964.

Zarlino, Gioseffo. *The Art of Counterpoint,* translated by Guy A. Marco and Claude V. Palisca. New Haven and London: Yale University Press, 1968.

Bibliography

Articles

Barbieri, Patrizio. "Gli ingegnosi cembali e 'violicembali' inventati da Juan Caramuel Lobkowitz per Ferdinando III (c. 1650): notizie inedite dal manoscritto Musica." Vigevano: Comune di Vigevano, 1990, pp. 91–112.

———. "Juan Caramuel Lobkowitz (1606–1682): Über die musikalischen Logarithmen und das Problem der musikalischen Temperatur." *Musiktheorie,* Volume 2, 1987, pp. 145–168.

———. "La sambuca lincea di Fabio Colonna e il tricembalo di Scipione Stella," in *La musica a Napoli durante il Seicento,* D. A. d'Alessandro and A. Ziino, editors. Rome: Torre d'Orefeo, 1987, pp. 167–216.

———. "An Unknown Fifteenth-Century French Manuscript on Organ Building and Tuning." *Organ Yearbook,* Volume 20, 1989, pp. 5–27.

———. "Violin Intonation: A Historical Survey." *Early Music,* Volume 19, February 1991, pp. 69–88.

Barnes, John. "Bach's Keyboard Temperament." *Early Music,* Volume 7, No. 2, April 1979, pp. 236–249.

Fenton, James. "How Great Art Was Made." *New York Review of Books,* Volume 45, No. 7, April 23, 1998, pp. 22–24, 26.

Hayes, Deborah. "Christian Huygens and the Science of Music." *Musicology at the University of Colorado,* Volume 1, No. 1, December 1977, pp. 17–31.

Hooke, Robert. "A Curious Dissertation." London: *Philosophical Transactions,* December 19, 1727.

Kuttner, Fritz A. "Prince Chu Tsai-Yü's Life and Work, a Reevaluation of his Contribution to the Equal Temperament Theory." *Ethnomusicology,* Volume 19, No. 2, May 1975, pp. 163–206.

Lindley, Mark. "Mersenne on Keyboard Tuning." *Journal of Music Theory,* Volume 24, No. 2, Fall 1980, pp. 167–203.

Warren, Charles W. "Brunelleschi's Dome and Dufay's Motet." *Musical Quarterly,* Volume 59, 1973, pp. 92–105.

Wells, Robin Headlam. "John Dowland and Elizabethan Melancholy." *Early Music,* Volume 13, No. 4, November 1985, pp. 514–528.

Wright, Craig. "Dufay's *Nuper rosarum flores,* King Solomon's Temple, and the Veneration of the Virgin." Journal of the American Musicological Society, Volume 47, 1994, pp. 395–441.

Recordings

Blackwood, Easley. *Microtonal.* Chicago: Cedille Records CDR 90000 018, 1994.

Index

Index

Index

Index

Index

Index

Index

Index

Index

Illustration Credits

A Note About the Author

Stuart Isacoff is a pianist, composer, lecturer, and critic and founding editor of the magazine *Piano Today*. He is a recipient of the prestigious ASCAP Deems Taylor Award for excellence in writing about music. His articles have appeared in the *New York Times*, *The New Grove Dictionary of Music in America*, *Chamber Music*, *Musical America*, *Stagebill*, *Symphony*, and *Connoisseur*. Mr. Isacoff has published many original musical compositions and is the author of several instructional books.

He has taught at Brooklyn College of the City University of New York; William Paterson University in Wayne, New Jersey; and the Verbier Festival and Academy in Verbier, Switzerland. As a recitalist he has performed at the Verbier Festival; the Van Cliburn Piano Institute in Fort Worth, Texas; the Gilmore International Keyboard Festival in Kalamazoo, Michigan; the Gina Bachauer International Piano Foundation in Salt Lake City, Utah; the Caramoor Center for the Arts in Katonah, New York; and the Greenwich House Music School in New York City. He lives with his wife and two daughters in Bergen County, New Jersey.

A Note on the Type

This book was set in Monotype Dante, a typeface designed by Giovanni Mardersteig (1892–1977). Conceived as a private type for the Officina Bodoni in Verona, Italy, Dante was originally cut only for hand composition by Charles Malin, the famous Parisian punch cutter, between 1946 and 1952. Its first use was in an edition of Boccaccio's *Trattatello in laude di Dante* that appeared in 1954. The Monotype Corporation's version of Dante followed in 1957. Although modeled on the Aldine type used for Pietro Cardinal Bembo's treatise *De Aetna* in 1495, Dante is a thoroughly modern interpretation of the venerable face.

Composed by North Market Street Graphics, Lancaster, Pennsylvania

Printed and bound by Quebecor World, Fairfield, Pennsylvania

Designed by Ralph Fowler